Gamification by Design
Implementing Game Mechanics in
Web and Mobile Apps

Gamification by Design

Implementing Game Mechanics in
Web and Mobile Apps

Gabe Zichermann and Christopher Cunningham

O'REILLY®

Beijing · Cambridge · Farnham · Köln · Sebastopol · Tokyo

Gamification by Design
by Gabe Zichermann and Christopher Cunningham

Published by O'Reilly Media, Inc., 1005 Gravenstein Highway North, Sebastopol, CA 95472.

O'Reilly books may be purchased for educational, business, or sales promotional use. Online editions are also available for most titles (*safari.oreilly.com*). For more information, contact our corporate/institutional sales department: 800-998-9938 or *corporate@oreilly.com*.

Editor: Mary Treseler

Production Editor: Kristen Borg

Copyeditor: Marlowe Shaeffer

Proofreader: Kristen Borg

Indexer: Ellen Troutman Zaig

Cover Designer: Mark Paglietti

Interior Designer: Ron Bilodeau

Illustrator: Robert Romano

Printing History:

August 2011: First Edition.

978-1-449-39767-8

[TI]

This book is dedicated to the designers of the scavenger hunt, tag, bridge, chess, poker, and solitaire. We may never know your names, but you truly made the world a whole lot more fun.

Contents

Preface

Gamification may be a new term, but the idea of using game-thinking and game mechanics to solve problems and engage audiences isn't exactly new. The military has been using games and simulations for hundreds (if not thousands) of years, and the U.S. military has been a pioneer in the use of video games across branches. Three hundred years ago, Scottish philosopher David Hume laid the groundwork for understanding player motivation with his views on the primacy of the irrational self. Since the 1960s, authors have been writing books that explore the "gamey" side of life and psychology, while since at least the 1980s, Hollywood has been hot on the trail of gamification with movies like *War Games*.

And behind all this is our general love affair with games themselves. Play and games are enshrined in our cultural record, emerging with civilizations, always intertwined. We are also now coming to understand that we are hardwired to play, with researchers increasingly discovering the complex relationships between our brains, neural systems, and game play (hint: play and games help you get smarter, faster). There's even an emerging scientific idea that games can help you live longer by staving off dementia and improving general health.

Therefore, seeing business and product designers embrace the concept of gamification should come as no surprise. As our society becomes more and more game-obsessed, much of the conventional wisdom about how to design products and market to consumers is no longer absolute. To further engage our audiences, we need to consider reward structures, positive reinforcement, and subtle feedback loops alongside mechanics like points, badges, levels, challenges, and leaderboards.

When done well, gamification helps align our interests with the intrinsic motivations of our players, amplified with the mechanics and rewards that make them come in, bring friends, and keep coming back. Only by carefully unpacking consumer emotions and desires can we design something that really sticks—and only through the power of gamification can we make that experience predictable, repeatable, and financially rewarding.

We wrote this book to help demystify some of the core concepts of game design as they apply to business, written from the perspective of what a marketer, product designer, product manager, or strategist would want to know. In that regard, we are indebted to the work of notable game designers who helped clarify and amplify the process of game design, making it into a quantifiable art and science. We have leveraged their work and refined the concepts to focus on those elements that are most relevant to business. We extracted good and bad patterns from both famous and lesser-known case studies, and we tested our concepts on countless (valiant) real-world customers to arrive at the set of demonstrable, high-impact ideas presented in this book.

When used together with the Gamification Master Class (also available from O'Reilly, at *http://oreilly.com/catalog/0636920017622*) and the supplemental videos, exercises, challenges, and resources available at *http://GamificationU.com*, this book becomes even more powerful. You can take a concept for gamifying your product, service, or idea and bring it to fruition using the techniques we describe. *Gamification by Design* takes a unique approach to this exciting, fast-moving, and powerful trend, and makes it practical. We hope you'll find it as useful as we enjoyed writing it.

Acknowledgments

We want to recognize the game-design writing and work of key thinkers, including Jesse Schell's *The Art of Game Design: A Book of Lenses* (Morgan Kaufmann), Jon Radoff's *Game On* (Wiley), and Ralph Koster's *A Theory of Fun for Game Design* (Paraglyph Press). We are also lucky to have been able to access and distill the insights of Sebastian Deterding, Susan Bonds, Jane McGonigal, Amy Jo Kim, Ian Bogost, Nick Fortugno, Nicole Lazzaro, Rajat Paharia, Kris Duggan, Keith Smith, and Tim Chang. And a special thanks to the folks at Badgeville who sponsored Chapter 8, providing insight into their groundbreaking product, as well as practical coding and design tips that can be used in any implementation.

We'd also like to recognize the efforts of Jeff Lopez, Danyell Thillet, and Joselin Linder, who each contributed in their own way by helping us research, refine, and produce this work. And, of course, to the O'Reilly Media team, including Mary Treseler, Sara Peyton, Kirk Walter, Keith (Steve) Thompson, and Betsy Waliszewski.

Gabe would like to thank his mother, father, (not-evil) stepdad, sister, and brother (why say in-law?), without whose support none of this would have been possible. Also, thanks to Veronica Cseke and the Fraizingers (Mary, Izzy, Rochelle, Shoshanna, and Elliot)—proof that family need not always be related by blood. And extra special thanks to Jason Evege, one of the most driven and inspirational people he's ever met.

Christopher would like to thank his family, especially his mother and father, for their limitless patience and encouragement of a child who would never stop asking questions—and then debating the answers. And special thanks to Pablo López Yáñez, for always supporting and encouraging an adult who hasn't changed all that much.

—New York City, 2011

Introduction

Summer. At dusk, children run between trees and fireflies, shouting through laughter and squealing, "You're it!"

Math class is ending. A cheer erupts as the teacher tells her students to put their books away. She splits the class into teams. In twos, they approach the chalkboard and face off for the love of numbers and grade-school honor.

It's Saturday night. A roomful of suburban mothers are playing Mahjong. As the tiles click and scores get recorded, they laugh, complain, and bond.

It is no wonder that the simple idea of a game can induce some of life's strongest and most satisfying memories. After childhood, games were relegated to the fringes of our lives—the downtime, the fun between the drudgery of work, the opposite of real life.

But the tides are turning. Games have begun to influence our lives every day. They affect everything from how we vacation to how we train for marathons, learn a new language, and manage our finances. What we once called "play" at the periphery of our lives is quickly becoming the way we interact. Games are the future of work, fun is the new "responsible," and the movement that is leading the way is gamification.

Gamification

Bandied about as the marketing buzzword of our time, gamification can mean different things to different people. Some view it as making games explicitly to advertise products or services. Others think of it as creating 3D virtual worlds that drive behavioral change or provide a method for training users in complex systems.

They are all correct. Gamification brings together all the disparate threads that have been advanced in games for nongaming contexts. In this way, we unite concepts such as serious games, advergaming, and games-for-change into a cohesive worldview that's informed by the latest research into behavioral psychology and the success of social games.

For our purposes we will define the term gamification as follows:

> The process of game-thinking and game mechanics to engage users and solve problems.

This framework for understanding gamification is both powerful and flexible—it can readily be applied to any problem that can be solved through influencing human motivation and behavior.

Take broccoli consumption. There are a lot of children in the world that consider broccoli to be a real problem. In fact, 70% of us have a gene that makes it taste bitter. This genetic adaptation (found on gene Htas2r38) is likely linked to the fact that cruciferous vegetables (which include broccoli and cabbage, among others) historically blocked the uptake of iodine to the thyroid. Thus, in environments with low amounts of natural iodine, our perception of bitterness in these vegetables actually once protected us.

It took about 10,000 years to domesticate these vegetables so they became safe to eat. However, statistics show that it takes the average child 12 years to go from hating broccoli to loving it. And research shows that if you possess the Htas2r38 gene, you still perceive the bitterness—even into adulthood. So what has changed? Certainly not the broccoli-eating taste buds. Yet something is different, and that difference lies in perception. The palate changes, and bitter is no longer bad.

But what if we wanted to change kids' minds about eating broccoli in fewer than a dozen years? We could certainly force them to eat the vegetable, but they would be likely to strongly dislike or rebel against the order. We could try to convince them to like it using facts, reasoning against their taste buds, or with social proof—"Mikey likes it"—but these methods are unreliable.

The two workable approaches—used by parents for generations—are to make a game out of it (e.g., the "airplane" landing) or to slather the broccoli with cheese sauce. Approach #1 tends to stop working after a while—there are only so many airplanes a child will consent to land. And approach #2 tends to produce a love of cheese sauce, and outweighs the health benefits of getting the kid to eat broccoli in the first place.

The obvious solution is to combine the two ideas. Make eating the broccoli both more fun (with a little game) and more rewarding (with a little cheese sauce, or dessert afterwards). The interplay among challenge, achievement, and reward not only allows you to train children to eat their broccoli, but it releases dopamine in the brain, intrinsically reinforcing the action as biologically positive.

In other words, by turning the experience into a game—including some reward for achievement—we can produce unprecedented behavior change. And when we amplify this loop with social proof and feedback, the sky's the limit for viral growth. Heck, your kids might even show their friends how to turn broccoli into dopamine and chocolate cake (for dessert, and only after they eat their veggies) if you're lucky…and good.

Or, consider a surprisingly similar but business-related challenge: professional service marketplaces. There are numerous online sites—including major sites like oDesk (*http://odesk.com*) and specialized ones like Behance (*http://behance.com*)—that help marketers connect with skilled developers, and where competition for customers and the best practitioners can be fierce. Once the novelty of marketplaces wears off, how do the respective parties decide to choose one over the other? How do the markets ensure loyalty and engagement among their fickle and price-conscious users?

One such marketplace, DevHub (*www.devhub.com*), thinks it's found the answer: gamification. By deploying some of the basic tenets of the discipline—and with the judicious use of game mechanics such as points, badges, levels, challenges, and rewards—DevHub has quickly differentiated itself as a market leader. The company has raised various engagement metrics, such as time on site, by as much as 20% over pregamified levels. With a clear emphasis on making things more fun and rewarding, DevHub has broken the dour cycle of quoting, bidding, coding, and follow-up necessary to run a successful web project.

Make no mistake, the core work is unchanged, and nothing has fundamentally shifted in the mechanics of designing a website. Only the perceptions of DevHub's users have been altered—for the better. Understanding our potential to experience the same things in two ways is the first step to understanding the power of gamification.

Engagement

The term "engagement," in a business sense, indicates the connection between a consumer and a product or service. Unsurprisingly, the term is also used to name the period in a romantic couple's relationship during which they are preparing and planning to spend the rest of their lives together. Engagement is the period of time at which we have a great deal of connection with a person, place, thing, or idea.

There is no single metric on the Web or in mobile technology that breaks down or sufficiently measures engagement. Page views and unique viewers don't quite answer the question of who is engaging with our products, services, ideas, websites, and businesses as a whole.

We would be better off thinking of engagement as being comprised of a series of potentially interrelated metrics that combine to form a whole. These metrics are:

- Recency
- Frequency
- Duration
- Virality
- Ratings

Collectively, they can be amalgamated as an "E" (or engagement) score. The relative proportion, or importance, of each of these metrics will vary depending on the type of business you are in. For example, a café might care more about frequency and recency, but less about duration; whereas a dating site may live or die by the duration of each interaction. See Figure I-1 for an image of this concept.

The importance of E is obvious given the current prevailing theory. What is being proved as we move toward a more peer-to-peer, viral, and social marketing environment is that traditional brand marketing isn't working anymore.

Rather than the antiquated idea of pushing consumers to "buy more!", engaging users in order to generate revenue is the marketing model of the future. Simply put, engagement does not follow revenue. Instead, behind engagement, revenue follows.

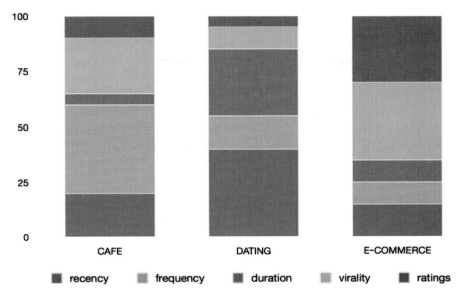

Figure I-1. *Some sample E proportions that might be appropriate in the contexts of a café, a dating site, and e-commerce.*

This is clearly demonstrated in the model of hugely successful social game companies such as Zynga. One of their key innovations in the field of marketing is that Zynga views customers in terms of a funnel, with a large potential target population at the top. Those users are generally not paying to interact with a product, service, or brand, but as they progress down the funnel, users are self-selected based on engagement. Their corresponding spending and commitment to the experience increase in tandem. In this model, the most loyal customers pay the most, while the average (or novice user) is being slowly drawn into the ecosystem. It is a reversal of the classic customer acquisition and loyalty model, and a very powerful view.

Note. *Did you know that in a typical social game, more than 90% of the users don't pay anything at all? The remaining group may pay thousands of dollars per month to play, based on their level of engagement. But no matter which group you're in, the social game designer considers you a player.*

Loyalty

The word most frequently used to describe engagement, particularly in a marketing context, is loyalty. In fact, to a great extent, engagement and loyalty are synonymous. However, when you hear the word "loyalty," it conjures up several meanings. One meaning is the type of loyalty that a dog feels toward his master—an unfailing obedience that allows the dog's owner to do no wrong in the eyes of the pet. However, blind acquiescence is not the kind of loyalty we're interested in developing throughout this book, and is a fool's errand in most business contexts. With few exceptions, we cannot and likely should not attempt to get absolute fealty from our users.

What we will look at is a form of loyalty that gets users to make incremental choices in your favor when all things are mostly equal. When products, price, or place are grossly unequal, gamification—and the loyalty it engenders—is much less meaningful. But when you have great product-market fit, gamification can provide a powerful accelerant to your efforts.

As with broccoli and children, if given enough time and incentive, we can overcome our natural programming. Not to put too fine a point on it, but why wait?

What Gamification Isn't

As we begin our journey into what gamification can do, we also need to be clear about what it cannot do. At least in the scope of this book, gamification is not merely about slapping some badges on your website; you need to take a more thoughtful approach, as advocated here. Also, if you expect gamification to fix your business' core problems—bad products or poor product-market fit—it will not.

Moreover, this book will not help you build a world where your consumer's avatar is chasing gremlins with an AK-47 in order to save the spaghetti sauce your company is trying to sell in outer space. It will also not teach you how to build a Facebook game where users match colored jewels to get discounts on insurance. While these may be viable options for some businesses (in 2003), we posit they are not really the best techniques for building long-term engagement or loyalty. Simply put, building actual games-with-a-capital-G is not this book's purpose.

Instead, we will share an understanding of the design process used by some of the world's biggest brands and hottest startups to gamify their customer interactions. We'll start by looking at what drives users to play and the core psychology that makes games so compelling. We'll separate the wheat from the chaff within the social and video game design rubric, and share what's relevant from the discipline with you, the builder. And finally, we'll show you—in concrete terms—how to architect and implement various core elements of gamification on the Web and mobile platforms, including some practical implementation concepts from one of the world's leading gamification technology pioneers.

Our objective is to give you the tools, techniques, and process-thinking you'll need to design gamification into your unique experience. It's not unlike learning how to bake—and a cake metaphor is apt considering the dialogue about gamification today. While we can spread gamified "icing" on your product or service with relative ease, unless the underlying cake is also delicious, most users won't want to take a second bite. Exactly the way a great baker creates treats through the interplay of structure and sweetness, so too must a well-designed gamified site marry substance with reward.

To achieve this, we will explore how—with a keen understanding of your customer — baking gamification into your business can produce the ideal product. Through the basics of gamification, player motivation, game mechanics, and their implementation, you will be handed the recipe that will take your business from everyday to gamified. We're going to make something absolutely irresistible.

Put on your apron, and hold on to your toque. Gamification is about to change everything.

CHAPTER 1

Foundations

As we mentioned in the Introduction, game mechanics cannot solve fundamental business problems. It will not rebuild poor infrastructure, nor will it heal disastrous customer service. And unless your actual business purpose is making games, it is unlikely that the result of gamification will give your product the full viral power of Zynga's Facebook games, such as *FarmVille* and *CityVille*.

As you arrive at the concept of gamification, you might bring with you even more preconceived ideas. For example, perhaps you believe that location-based services like Foursquare serve no real purpose beyond their game elements. Simply put, Foursquare allows players to "check in" at locations using mobile devices, and in doing so the player can earn badges, signal their location to friends, and keep track of where they've been. If someone checks in at a location more than any other player, he is deemed "mayor" of the establishment and is recognized as such by fellow players, the business, and the game itself. But as we delve into this sweeping phenomenon, it will be clear that there is more on the line than badges and mayorships—the desire to be *connected* drives the player's location-based journey.

To some extent, it is the sheer simplicity of Foursquare and similar games that have made them successful. Gamification can fix large-scale, complex problems, but that doesn't mean its application needs to be large-scale and complex. Gamification that is simple, rewarding, and fun can be equally or more effective. And in focusing on game mechanics that meet these criteria, you will be amazed by how much can be accomplished.

Finally, for the purposes of this book, we are going to try and refrain from using the terms "customer" or "user," and instead use the word "player" from this point forward. By thinking of our clients as players, we shift our frame of mind toward their engagement with our products and services. Rather than looking at the immediacy of a single financial transaction, we are considering a long-term and symbiotic union wrapped in a ribbon of fun.

The Fun Quotient

Let's start here: everything has the potential to be fun.

Perhaps you're thinking, "No way. How about going to the dentist? Going to the dentist isn't fun!"

Or maybe your first thought is, "Waiting in line is boring. Waiting in a line is the opposite of fun."

We're sure you can think of an endless array of things in life that are just not fun. Surgery, for example, or changing a baby's dirty diaper, or clipping someone else's toenails. However, some of the most popular games of the past five years have used incredibly banal ideas as their thematic hooks. In fact, four of the most popular games in the past decade include such thrilling activities as planting crops (*FarmVille*), waiting tables (*Diner Dash*), diapering a baby (*Diaper Dash*), and doing other people's hair and nails (*Sally's Salon*).

Another highly rated online game has its players perform one of the most stressful jobs in our society (which boasts one of the highest career-related suicide rates in the entire world): air traffic control. In the blockbuster game *Flight Control* (see Figure 1-1), players are expected to guide airplanes safely to a runway without killing any of the hundreds of passengers onboard.

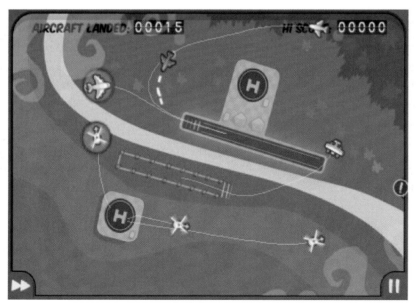

Figure 1-1. Flight Control is an immensely popular iOS game that puts you in the shoes of an air traffic controller—a high-stress job. Why is this concept fun?

So, why did these brazen game designers pitch games based on banal activities to a room full of executives? And why didn't every single one of them get laughed out of the building? The answer is simple: it is the mechanics of a game—not the theme—that make it fun.

At any casino in the world, a player is overwhelmed by myriad slot machines. From *Wheel of Fortune* to Harley-Davidson, slot machine branding is as outwardly different as a juicy steak is to a bunch of organic carrots. But the machines are not different. In fact, other than the logo, those machines are almost identical mechanically: push the button, pull the arm, and let the cherries align to win. With all due respect to *Wheel of Fortune*, it is not the game show's logo that keeps players at those machines—it's the underlying mechanics.

This does not mean that the brand is an unimportant feature. In fact, it is the way we dress the game mechanics that attracts most people to pull that lever in the first place. While some might think that nearly killing hundreds of imaginary passengers in an air traffic control-related incident is as exciting as it gets, others will be drawn in by the muscled heroes of a Harlequin romance novel. Although the underlying game mechanics hook the player, what brought each of them into the experience was different—and more than likely made to pique a particular interest.

Fun Is Job #1

In the past 20 years, there have been no major blockbusters in educational software/games—the field otherwise known as *edutainment*. Software focused on children, the demographic with the biggest claims on fun, are not getting it where they arguably need it most—in learning. Does this mean that it's impossible to educate by having fun? Is school forever consigned to be boring?

The famous geography game *Where in the World Is Carmen Sandiego?* (see Figure 1-2) was the last blockbuster hit in educational games. It was inarguably a tremendously fun way to learn about country and province capitals, as well as the major exports and waterways of places far removed from the classroom. Since then, thousands of educational software companies have attempted and failed to create another sensation.

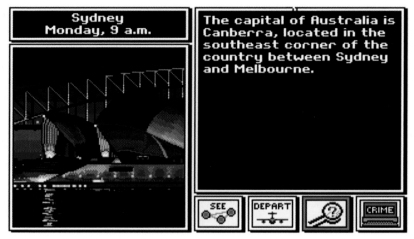

Figure 1-2. "Where in the World Is Carmen Sandiego?" is among the best-selling educational games of all time, and was popular among teachers, parents, and students alike.

So, where in the world is the next big hit? Games aligning entertainment and education like *Civilization* and *SimCity* have taught millions of people history lessons and the basics of urban planning. These are not pedagogical games. They weren't designed to be educational. But they use history and real city schema as a backdrop to explain ideas; thus, education becomes a byproduct of fun.

This is precisely the opposite of what has happened to educational software. In fact, once teachers and parents got involved, they systematically extracted the fun from the game. Kids could smell that shift from fun to work a mile away. And Carmen Sandiego's position as the last megahit of edutainment is mostly a reflection of this simple fact: it was the last time parents, teachers, and children agreed on a video game. (To be fair, some companies have had limited success building educational games in specific verticals.)

So, can children learn from games? Absolutely. Research by Dr. Arne May at Germany's University of Regensburg clearly showed that learning a new task produces a demonstrable increase in the brain's gray matter in mere weeks. And brain scientists the world over agree that games' challenge-achievement-reward loop promotes the production of dopamine in the brain, reinforcing our desire to play.

The real question then, is: will children learn from a game if it is not fun? Judging by the state of the educational software industry, they will not. In other words, if you start with the education and put fun second, learning doesn't seem to work the same way—or as effectively.

Note. *Want to learn more about the state of educational games? Meet inspirational teachers—like Ananth Pai, shown in Figure 1-3—and see how they're using games and gamification to change behavior. Visit GamificationU.com to get exclusive videos and exercises, and to interact with the experts.*

Figure 1-3. Ananth Pai is a pioneer in gamifying education. Visit GamificationU.com to see videos and get more information about Mr. Pai and his work.

The Evolution of Loyalty

Loyalty, as we've already mentioned, will be defined for our purposes as encouraging an incremental choice in your favor when all things are mostly equal. Loyalty and consumerism share a long and varied history. While there are likely ancient examples of loyalty programs in one form or another, we will begin with loyalty programs in America.

With the growth of urban centers in the 19th century, markets and local merchants began to thrive. People arriving in town to buy their weekly supplies were often plied by one seller or another to buy, for example, 10 pounds of sugar and get their next pound free. Thus a 10:1 ratio came to form the basic structure of loyalty programs. In fact, it is such a canonical example that 95% of all loyalty programs today remain "buy 10 get 1 free." Figure 1-4 shows a slight variation offered at Café Nero.

Figure 1-4. Café Nero's novel approach is to offer buy nine, get one free.

The problem with this model is that it gives things away for free to the people most likely to pay you regardless. Social game designers do not abide by this fundamental flaw. While there is nothing wrong with offering a reward or thanks to your most loyal players, their purchasing habits might not be negatively affected without the freebie. However, new or novice customers certainly will be affected. Over time, an excessive dependence on "free stuff" or discounts habituates players to constantly expect that as a condition of purchase.

The 10:1 model remained the standard until the 1930s when S&H Green Stamps was launched. S&H's program allowed participating merchants to reward players with stamps when those players made specific purchases. Those stamps, shown in Figure 1-5, were then collected in a book. Once filled, those books could be redeemed for free stuff from a catalog or at an S&H Green Stamp store (at various rates, depending on the desired product).

Figure 1-5. S&H Green Stamps brought a "virtual currency" to retail in the 1930s.

What S&H understood was that with the introduction of a virtual currency, people lose track of value. They can no longer identify how much those individual stamps are worth. While "buy 10 pounds of sugar, get 1 free" precisely values that free pound of sugar, with the advent of Green Stamps, valuation became vague. Buying a shirt earns you 16 Green Stamps, and pants are worth 20. A transistor radio is valued at 60, but a trip to Hawaii is 6,420. How much is that stamp worth, again?

While consumers had little concept of value exchange, S&H knew exactly how much those stamps were worth at any time. Thus, the first virtual currency was created.

Loyalty programs continued in a similar fashion until 1981. First, American Airlines introduced AAdvantage, followed in short order by United's Mileage Plus and TWA's Aviator. With the development of the frequent-flyer program, businesses discovered that loyalty is less about free stuff than it is about status. If you've ever tried to redeem miles for a summertime vacation in Europe, you understand immediately that the free flights are not the core of the system's value proposition.

In fact, people are quick to make the connection that joining one of these programs means standing in a shorter line for just about everything. They also understand that players get more upgrades, faster phone and Internet customer help, and better overall service. None of these things costs the business much, but each one powerfully drives brand loyalty among their players. Figure 1-6 displays such loyalty programs across a range of products, from airlines to rental car companies to grocery stores.

Figure 1-6. Airline loyalty programs, launched in the 1980s, shifted the focus to status.

Frequent-flyer programs remained the best loyalty program model until recently, when virtual rewards systems began popping up online and on mobile devices. A game such as *FarmVille* doesn't even pretend to offer real-world prizes. There are no faster lines, no five books of stamps for a model airplane, no free bags of sugar. In fact, the notion of redemption of any kind has been dropped completely. No redemption. Not a pin, not a cup of coffee. Nothing. The cost of producing customer loyalty has dropped precipitously. It used to be 10 cents on the dollar—buy 10 get 1 free. Now, for applications like *FarmVille* or Foursquare, costs are nearly zero.

At the same time, the value of status is rising. In the old days (pre-2008) if a person preferred Cuisinart over KitchenAid, for example, how was that bias expressed? How did she get her friends to understand this loyalty choice? First, her friends needed to be standing in the kitchen near the product itself. Then, a conversation would have to introduce the subject. This process was called *word of mouth marketing*.

In short, the message of the word of mouth marketing industry was: build a great product and consumers will talk about it. There was no process, and word of mouth marketing was a hit-driven business.

Alternatively, a company like Zynga has a very good idea of how their word of mouth marketing works, because it's part of the phenomenon of social networking. On Twitter and Facebook, players of *FarmVille* constantly express their loyalty by posting about the game, inviting other people, and working to improve their play experience through baked-in social rewards. If your product is not in this social media "loyalty stream," it is not part of the discussion. Loyalty is no longer private. It is no longer a matter of standing in a kitchen next to your favorite mixer. It is public, and millions are viewing it.

Status at the Wheel

In the fourth season of the show *Deal or No Deal*, a young woman finally won the coveted million-dollar prize by randomly selecting the suitcase in which it was contained. If asked, you probably couldn't think of her name—even though it took four seasons of the popular game show for someone to get that win.

Another reality-show contest winner has a decidedly more familiar name. Christian Siriano is a fashion designer and the winner of the fourth cycle of the Heidi Klum–hosted series, *Project Runway*. If you don't know his name, perhaps you know his catchphrase—when displeased with something, Siriano refers to it as "a hot mess," a phrase that has since entered the American vernacular.

Whereas the million-dollar winner of *Deal or No Deal* came and went as quickly as a buxom blond opened the suitcase, Christian Siriano's name has remained. What was his prize? $100,000. With his winnings he can't afford to start a fashion line in New York City, Paris, or London. Let's be honest, he can't even afford more than a few items of high-end clothing for that amount of money.

Similarly, the winners of *Top Chef*, *Hell's Kitchen*, and *Chopped* all compete for negligible prizes: a *Chopped* champion brings in a mere $10,000, and *Hell's Kitchen* winners get a job as their prize where, ostensibly, they will need to continue working for Gordon Ramsay (that's some prize!). So, what are these players really competing for? It is unlikely they are taking themselves away from their families and undergoing rigorous competition over the course of months in order to win a little money and some steak knives. What is their motivation? What did Christian Siriano get when the camera's turned off?

After the show, Siriano went on to design a 15-piece collection for Puma, develop a make-up line for Victoria's Secret, and write a book. While his stint on *Project Runway* did not win him riches, it granted him fame, recognition, and status in spades.

If you don't have a ton of cash to give away as an incentive (who does?), status is an excellent alternative. It is a great driver of loyalty, not to mention a player's fiscal behavior (and, over time, you can bet it is a whole lot cheaper). A gamified program with a status benefit needs far fewer monetary, physical, or even real-world-redeemable rewards. Status is, as American Airlines understood in 1981—and most of us clearly grok today— an extremely powerful reward. But is it everything?

SAPS

SAPS is an acronym that stands for status, access, power, and stuff. Simply put, it is a system of rewards. Conveniently, it lists each potential prize in order from the most to the least desired, the most sticky to the least sticky, and the cheapest to the most expensive.

Status

Status is the relative position of an individual in relation to others, especially in a social group. Status benefits and rewards give players the ability to move ahead of others in a defined ranking system. Importantly, this ranking system need not be based on the real world at all—it works perfectly in a purely constructed environment. Some examples of status items include badges and leaderboards. Although we talk about them in greater detail in future chapters, here is a brief introduction to these two core mechanics that affect and measure status:

Badges

> Badges are a known status item. They can be given out virtually or physically. However, they must be visible to other players in the game; otherwise, their meaning and valuation is limited.

Levels and leaderboards

Levels and leaderboards are another way to indicate that a player has more or less status or achievement in a given game; they can be a powerful tool in your quest for engagement.

Access

Gilt Groupe (*www.gilt.com*) is a social website geared toward flash sales of high-end fashion. The top 1% of Gilt players receive a scented candle and card in the mail as part of their induction into Gilt's top-tier loyalty program, Gilt Noir. Other than this package shown in Figure 1-7 (with a retail value of less than $30), these top players' prize is a 15-minute head start for all sales. For Gilt, the prize doesn't cost a thing. But to the player, that extra time to pull in the best bargains is exceptionally meaningful, because supplies in each sale are limited.

Figure 1-7. Gilt Noir gives top buyers 15 minutes of early access in online flash sales, as well as this lovely welcome package.

Consider how seemingly revolutionary this is in the context of most loyalty programs. Instead of offering top customers discounts or giveaways, Gilt Noir members are given early access. This is a process-driven version of the informal programs long at work at high-end fashion houses like Bottega Veneta or Gucci, where top buyers and celebrities get first dibs on cool new products.

Other ways to provide access as a reward to your players can include lunch with a CEO, priority or VIP seating, or the earliest possible appointments.

Power

Awarding power to your players offers a modicum of control over other players in the game. For example, a good player might be asked to serve as a moderator on a forum.

Not only will players work for you for free, power benefits to them are huge. Most forums, as well as *World of Warcraft*, successfully offer positions of power for which their players vie on a daily basis.

Stuff

While this list indicates that "stuff" is the least important reward or prize, we are not against freebies. If you have great items to give away, and if players are expecting to receive free items, stuff can be a strong incentive.

Once the item has been given away, however, the incentive to play is finished. In other words, stuff is only good until it is redeemed, which is the exact length of time your players will engage in the game.

Of course, some might argue that they'd rather get, for example, a free ice cream than be badged "Ice Cream King," and, off the cuff, it's hard to disagree with that assessment. However, it is important to remember that, "off the cuff," no one is yet in the game. Once he is, the value of becoming an "Ice Cream King" might mean that he has reached a new level in game play that allows him to enter a contest to create a new ice cream flavor. Or, maybe it will allow him to skip to the front of the line every time he comes in to buy an ice cream cone.

It's always the depth of meaning of the game that matters, not the monetary value of the prize. Remember, no matter what that tangible prize is, you need to disclose its value (or be sure the value is inherently known to your most loyal customers). As a result, players tend to value the interaction accurately. To illustrate this point, say that a regular coffee drinker just earned her 11th latte for free. After buying 10 lattes for $2.50 each, she knows what the 11th is worth.

How do players value status, access, power, and stuff? They cannot accurately price those benefits, so—in general—they tend to overvalue them. For example, when assessing the importance of not having to wait in line, most people overvalue their time saved. Similarly, they don't know how to quantify the six minutes they got to meet and chat with Lady Gaga backstage after winning a call-in contest. But the gamification designer understands these values, and the price is almost always cheaper—and the reward stickier—than giving away free stuff.

The House Always Wins

That truism underlies the last basic lesson of games in the real world: no matter what the player thinks, the house will always win a well-designed game. Just as any honest casino manager will tell you, while the illusion of winning is vital to motivating use and play, actually winning is much harder than it seems.

Broadly speaking, this has implications not only for players, but also for those of us charged with building and designing great user experiences. As markets gamify and consumer demand for fun, engaging, and creative experiences increases, you have a fundamental choice: either be the house, or get played.

Trust us, you want to be the former.

 Note. *Want to dive deeper into understanding the foundations of gamification? Access exclusive videos, exercises, and discussions at GamificationU.com today.*

CHAPTER 2

Player Motivation

The player is at the root of gamification. In any system, the player's motivation ultimately drives the outcome. Therefore, understanding player motivation is paramount to building a successfully gamified system.

Let's Play a Game

Quick: grab a piece of paper or open a text document. Write down the three most fun things you did in the last two weeks. There are no right or wrong answers. Set your list aside until you've read this chapter. Then, revisit the list and ask yourself, "How similar am *I* to my canonical player?" Visit *http://GamificationU.com* for more exercises and supplementary materials to go along with this book.

We already know that games are generally good motivators. By focusing on three central components—pleasure, rewards, and time—games have become one of the most powerful forces in all of humanity. Uniquely, games are able to get people to take actions that they don't always know they want to take, without the use of force, in a predictable way.

Powerful Human Motivators

From Greek mythology to daytime soaps, it is clear that sex—or the drive to have it—will make a person do almost anything. Paris' abduction of the lovely Helen of Troy led King Menelaus to begin the Trojan War. So, like games, sex has the unusual ability to make people do things that are not necessarily in their best long-term interest. However, unlike games, sexual attraction is hard to predict and control, making it a less useful tool in engagement.

Similarly, violence can yield unparalleled coercive results. Putting a gun to a person's head will likely get him to accomplish any task you request. However, chances are he won't enjoy a second of it, and he certainly won't come back for more. The force fallacy—that punishment can accomplish great results—is a powerful, flawed belief.

Games, however, hit the sweet spot. They marry the desire-drive of sex with the predictability of duress—except without force and, when successful, driven entirely by enjoyment. This pattern is also why games have a dark side: people addicted to slot machines can look as though they haven't seen the sun in months, and *World of Warcraft* players are sometimes accused of neglecting their real-life duties for the sake of a virtual reality. But there is also a bright side to games, in that they are improving people's health, the way they learn, and the way they live.

The Force Fallacy and Gamification: Speed Camera Lottery

Speed cameras throughout the world are designed to quickly photograph speeders and send them a ticket in the mail along with the evidence of their crime. In many Nordic countries, penalties are based on the speeder's income, not the speed she was traveling at the time she was caught.

Against this backdrop, and as part of a competition called The Fun Theory, San Francisco-based game designer Kevin Richardson designed Speed Camera Lottery (see Figure 2-1). The concept is simple: instead of just issuing outsized penalties to speeders, photograph every car that passes the checkpoint, and those observing the limit are entered into a prize drawing to win the fines of the speeders. The modified camera gave instant positive feedback in the form of a thumbs up.

The effect was immediate—speed dropped at the checkpoint by an average of 20%, and consumers thought the idea was fantastic. This is a great example of game-thinking at work: turning a negative loop into a positive one for the greater good.

Flow

At the heart of the success of games is an idea called *flow*. Our understanding of flow is derived from the research of Mihaly Csikszentmihalyi, a psychology professor who is noted for his studies of happiness and creativity. Achieving flow—or being "in the zone"—indicates a player's state between anxiety and boredom, meeting his own motivational level in that experience.

When a jazz musician is playing her saxophone, or a runner is training for a race, she exists in a state of suspended animation. She is calm and focused. A writer, mid-stream in narrative, forgets the outside world for a moment. It is safe to suggest that almost everyone has had that experience of losing track of time and space while playing a game, cooking, working out, cleaning the house, or talking on the telephone.

Figure 2-1. Speed Camera Lottery turned speeding tickets into lottery tickets for drivers who obeyed the speed limit, reducing speeding and improving driver satisfaction.

Meanwhile, game designers are obsessed with creating this state. They are always looking for ways for the player to be at one with the game. It is a constant quest to bring someone within the system only to guide him, seamlessly, into the highly prized state of flow. But *how*?

The designer must create a careful interplay of system and player, relentlessly testing those interactions to find that point between anxiety and boredom, as depicted in Figure 2-2. There is a broad spectrum of psychological phenomena that becomes important in this process of guiding a player to master a system. One such phenomenon is reinforcement.

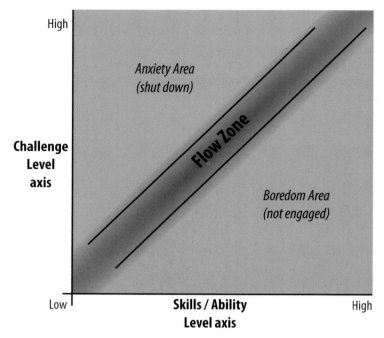

Figure 2-2. The state of flow is achieved when a player is placed between anxiety and boredom over a period of time.

Reinforcement

Reinforcement studies how we convert an expected reward into player action by varying the quantity and delivery schedule of that reward. Pioneered by researchers like Pavlov and B. F. Skinner, and extended into human studies, understanding the power of reinforcement is key to structuring the right reward systems.

If a mammal such as a lab rat is given a pellet of food once an hour, during the 59 minutes between receiving each pellet, the animal will invariably go off and do something else in its cage. Only at the 60th minute will it come back to get the dispensed pellet.

This structure is similar in form to many Industrial Era jobs. A worker gets a paycheck every two weeks. What happens in the interval between paychecks is completely aligned with that end result. In other words, the worker will only do exactly what is required of her during the days in between to ensure that she will get her biweekly direct deposit. No more, no less. This is called *fixed-interval reinforcement*. Not surprisingly, fixed-interval reinforcement schedules tend to yield low levels of engagement.

On the other end of the spectrum is variable ratio, variable schedule reinforcement. In this model, the lab rat doesn't know how big the reward will be or when it will happen, but it knows that at some point it will come. Therefore, that rat will press the dispensing pedal in its cage endlessly until it gets its reward. It is exactly the model used in slot machine gaming, as well as for almost every other archetypal gambling model. Another name for this behavior modifier is *operant conditioning*, and it is undeniably addictive to mammals. As illustrated in Figure 2-3, higher responses equal more engagement behaviors.

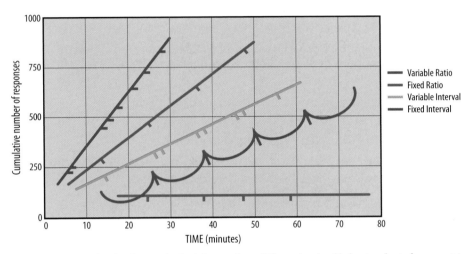

Figure 2-3. *Different kinds of reward schedules produce different levels of behavioral reinforcement in mammals.*

While operant-conditioning experiences can be dangerous and unappealing to many, using them judiciously within a broader game-like experience is a powerful force for driving player behavior. In practice, you should plan to include some amount of slot-style rewards in your experience, regardless of the context. The key is to not overuse their power.

But unlike rats in a cage, most humans are not required to play, let alone play with real engagement. So, what drives us to play in the first place?

Why People Play

A good working theory for why people are motivated to play games maintains that there are four underlying reasons, which can be viewed together or separately as individual motivators:

- For mastery

- To destress

- To have fun

- To socialize

In a 2004 paper entitled "Why We Play Games," Nicole Lazzaro, an expert on player experience and emotions in games, outlined four different kinds of fun:

Hard fun
> Where a player is trying to win some form of competition

Easy fun
> Where a player is focused on exploring the system

Altered state fun
> In which the game changes the way the player feels

Social fun
> During which the player engages with other players

In 1964, the famous social science best seller, *Games People Play* (Grove Press) by Eric Berne, M.D., exposed a series of games organically cultivated through common social interaction. The book, which focused heavily on the social engagement of "housewives" (an arguably outdated construct to be sure, but en vogue for its time), managed to recognize some interesting insights about social game play. In one of the book's most compelling examples, Berne talks about a game among the women whereby they go around and talk about the ways their husbands upset them: "He leaves his socks all over the place," one bemoans. "He hates my cooking," says another. "He forgets my birthday," laments a third.

But what would happen if someone in that circle chose not to play the game? According to Berne's research, if a fourth housewife says, "Actually, my husband is a good guy," there is a decisive and chastising consequence to her action. The fourth housewife won't get invited to the next party—plain and simple. The prize in this game is to win a follow-up invitation.

Berne leaves us with an emerging understanding of the social games that exist organically in the strata of our society. Even language indicates that we've been aware of these "hidden" games for some time: a person is called a "player" when he can get a lot of dates in the "dating game"; a government official "runs" for office in a "contest"; someone who is socially unsuccessful is labeled a "loser."

Exercise: Your Player's Story

Write the story of the canonical player of your game. As you design your system, you will focus on this player and what might appeal to him. What is his story—from his demographic to his psychographics? Write in one paragraph who he is.

Example Players:

Susan is a 32-year-old fifth grade teacher who lives in an urban community. She is mostly able to live within her means with the help of a credit card and, occasionally, her parents. She enjoys going out to clubs and concerts. She cooks for her friends and hosts dinner parties whenever she can. She is very fashion-conscious and easily spends a quarter of her paycheck on clothing and beauty products. She is obsessed with Facebook.

Chris is a 22-year-old recent college graduate who lives with three roommates in a suburban city. He works at a local radio station as a paid intern, as well as part time at a bar and grill as a line cook. He is in a band and is definitely interested in girls, although he'd trade a date in a second to hang out with any of his "boys." His favorite possession is easily his iPhone, although he would never admit it.

Ron is a 53-year-old salesman who listens to Rush Limbaugh or NPR—depending on who is telling the more entertaining story—during his many hours on the road. He also enjoys listening to jazz. He and his wife are planning to take a tour of Wine Country this fall. He is hardworking and motivated. He has two daughters who are doing well academically—one of whom is going to graduate high school at the end of the year. He worries about paying for college, although he's been saving for it since his children were small.

Player Types

The more you know about who is playing your game—both current and prospective players—the easier it is to design an experience that will drive their behavior in the desired way.

One rubric that can help you understand your players is to leverage the work accomplished by Richard Bartle in understanding player types. In his seminal work, developed by studying players of MMOGs (massively multiplayer online games), Bartle identified four types of players. Since then, the number has expanded from 4 to 8 to 16—however, the four types shown in Figure 2-4 remain arguably the stickiest, and therefore the most interesting for our purposes.

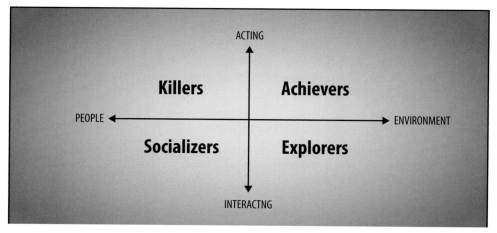

Figure 2-4. Bartle's player types.

Explorers

An explorer, in brief, likes to go out into the world in order to bring things back to his community and proclaim, "I discovered this thing!" In a sense, the experience *is* the objective. One example of a game suited to the explorer player type was *Super Mario Brothers* on the Nintendo Entertainment System. A player had to play 100 games or more to find every hidden level behind every pipe and block, and bring that knowledge back to his peers for kudos.

Achievers

People who like to achieve are an integral part of any competitive game. They drive a great deal of projects, services, and brands. The problem with designing exclusively for this player type is that it's difficult to develop a system where everyone can win and achieve. And for achievers, losing at the game will likely cause them to lose interest in playing it.

Moreover, a common bias we've observed when working with clients to gamify their experiences is that the majority of system, site, and product designers are high-achieving people. So, you naturally infer that the majority of players are similarly inclined. This turns out not to be true at all. The majority are socializers.

Socializers

This player type is made up of people who play games for the benefit of a social interaction. Games focused on socializers comprise some of the most enduring games throughout history—dominoes, bridge, mahjong, poker—the thread tying them together is that each is an extremely social experience. To be clear, it isn't that socializers don't care about the game or winning—they do. To them, the game is a backdrop for meaningful long-term social interactions. It's the context and catalyst, not the end in itself.

Killers

Also known as *griefers*, killers make up the smallest population of all of the player types. However, they are important to understand. They are similar to achievers in their desire to win; unlike achievers, however, winning isn't enough. They must win and someone else must lose. Moreover, killers really want as many people as possible to see the kill, and for their victims to express admiration/respect.

Bartle did not intend or develop these four player types to serve as a personality inventory. But with decades of game-thinking under our belts, it is easy to see how they can be useful when considering the players of gamified systems. And by placing the player types on an axis, we can see how they range from acting to interacting, and from people to environments.

 Note. *People are not exclusively one or another of the four player types. In fact, most people have some percentage of each. In all probability, a person's dominant player type changes throughout her life—and even varies from game to game. But it is a compelling way, as a game designer, to see how people are motivated to play and interact in a gamified system.*

If you take Bartle's test to figure out your player type, you will notice that, as we mentioned, they are mutually inclusive. In other words, a player can have characteristics of all four types at the same time. However, most people are not. For the average person, the breakdown might look something like this:

80% socializer

50% explorer

40% achiever

20% killer

If the scores were mutually exclusive, however, and a player could only be one type, we learn that the vast majority of people—as much as 75%—are probably socializers. In the context of the runaway success of games like *FarmVille* or poker, that statistic should not come as a particular surprise. Explorers and achievers each make up about 10% of the population, and killers account for 5%.

Note. *We're working with researchers at California State University, East Bay to turn Bartle's test into a personality inventory. Help define how gamer personalities mimic our personalities in the "real world." Visit GamificationU.com and click on the Bartle Test link for more info and to determine your player type.*

By bringing together many of the understandings we've developed in this chapter, the underpinnings of the social game movement suddenly become more apparent.

Social Games

The video games that have informed so much of our game-thinking over the last few years are actually the exception and not the rule. From the beginning of the modern computer/video game industry in the early 1970s until the 2000s, most titles were single-player or "two people in a room" multiplayer. So the new "social games" movement, led by titles such as *FarmVille*—and including slightly older games like *World of Warcraft*—really resemble the broad arc of historical games, rather than a new concept in itself. In fact, nearly all of our games throughout history—with the obvious exception of solitaire—have required other people to play.

Most game developers and technical designers are unlikely to resemble the players for whom they are designing. Like you, they tend to be an achievement-oriented breed, more so than the average person. It's a big bias to overcome when designing gamified systems. When they are thinking about game design, they are likely amassing points, seeking status, even killing to win. But they are not the average person.

The average person is looking to socialize—not win. Although achievements are nice to earn (and make players feel great), they are not the principal driver. If designers begin by thinking the game is about achievement, they will at some point realize they are excluding a big chunk of the audience. The average *World of Warcraft* player is as dependent on the guild (team) with which he fights his battles as he is on the battles themselves. Excusing himself from a family dinner to avoid letting down his team for a 7 p.m. raid is a far greater motivator than the raid itself. The raid could wait until after dinner. Most of society plays for the camaraderie and community of the game more than the actual win.

The Power of Team Play and Social Pressure

NextJump is a high-growth marketing company with a fitness-oriented CEO named Charlie Kim. In an effort to get the staff more fit (and reduce absenteeism/health care expenditures), Kim had gyms put into every office, and devised a novel challenge—the top employees checking in to workouts at the gym would split a cash prize. About 12% of the staff began to work out as a result of this offer. Then, NextJump changed the design, introducing geographically-based team play and leaderboards that pit the NYC office against Boston, and so on. Top teams this time split a similarly sized pot. Soon after the change, nearly 70% of NextJump's employees were working out regularly, mostly driven by each other to "not let the team down" and "beat the San Francisco office", etc. The power of team play to motivate users is—when done right—unparalleled.

Exercise: Rank Your Top Five Player Actions

You can download this and other exercises at *http://GamificationU.com*.

Before we can begin designing for engagement, we need to know what we want players to do—that is, what social actions we want them to take. This is best expressed in the form of social verbs. Rank the top five actions you most want your players to take. (You can also add your own actions, but be sure to use a verb form—but don't use "buy" or "consume".)

- Advocate
- Argue
- Comment
- Compare
- Compete
- Curare
- Explore
- Express

- Flirt
- Give
- Greet
- Harass
- Help
- Join
- Like
- Poke

- Rate
- Read
- Recommend
- Share
- Show off
- Taunt
- View
- Vote

Considering an auction website, here's an example ranking of your player's actions:

1. Compare
2. Explore
3. Show off
4. Compete
5. Rate

Intrinsic versus Extrinsic Motivation

Another aspect to understanding player motivations is by questioning where motivations come from. Broadly speaking, psychology has divided our motivations into two groups: intrinsic and extrinsic. Intrinsic motivations are those that derive from our core self and are not necessarily based on the world around us. Conversely, extrinsic motivations are driven mostly by the world around us, such as the desire to make money or win a spelling bee.

Exercise: Five Player Actions on Bartle's Chart

Once you've ranked the five most important actions for your service, place them on Bartle's player type chart. Where do the actions overlay on that chart? In the sample auction site we used in the previous sidebar, "Rank Your Top Five Player Actions," the list seems to focus on achievers/killers (compete, show off) and socializers (compare, rate), with a little bit in the explorers category (explore).

For an auction site, it makes sense that this is where most of the players fall. Collectors want to win the item. Sellers want to "win" as much money as possible. Especially in the last minute, an auction is very achievement/killer-oriented.

Take note if you don't have any actions in the socializer quadrant. You are probably missing something about the experience, which is problematic because socializers are the most universal type. You may not always have a lot of players who fall in the killer quadrant, but you will always have socializers.

If you are running a site dedicated to music, perhaps your list of actions and where they fall on Bartle's chart would be markedly different. You might find that more of your action points serve socializers and explorers, rather than achievers and killers. Music is an inherently social activity, but an explorer is drawn to the component of music that allows her to brag to her peers, "I discovered this musician."

Hint: If while doing this exercise you aren't developing a particular product or service, we suggest you imagine that you are creating for traders on the floor of the Chicago Board of Trade or a site for music lovers to talk about their favorite artists. Either way, think about the kinds of interactions that work best for your target player.

When it comes to intrinsic versus extrinsic motivation in a gamified or motivational design context, there are three schools of thought:

- In Daniel H. Pink's book *Drive* (Riverhead Trade), he attests that cash is a weak reward for getting players to complete complex tasks. The research he rounds up shows how an extrinsic motivator like cash doesn't work when people are given lateral-thinking tasks. In other words, when cash is introduced as a motivator, people's performance on creative or complex tasks drops. Thus, he contends that cash rewards are bad for incentivizing creative thought.

While we agree that cash is not always motivational and in some cases is actually demotivational, other extrinsic rewards can be astoundingly motivational for players. For example, long-term social status rewards can be particularly effective at nurturing creativity and play.

- Dr. John Houston, a preeminent researcher in competitiveness, found that exceptionally competitive people can be self-destructively competitive. His research showed that people—principally achiever/killer types—with a high level of competitiveness compete even when there is nothing to be gained. Moreover, they tend to compete even when there's a clear disincentive to do so. When told that they must collaborate with a partner, hyper-competitive people will continue to try and figure out how to win, even against a collaborator, even when there is nothing to win.

- Overjustification/replacement bias argues that replacing an intrinsic motivation with an extrinsic reward is a fairly easy thing to do. Research suggests that when a child who plays the piano simply because she enjoys it is introduced to competitive piano playing, many changes in her behavior can occur. For example, if she begins to win competitions, then subsequently loses, she will stop playing piano. That is, extrinsic rewards crush intrinsic motivation, which never returns. The challenge for overjustification as a design constraint is that it's not obvious that we care to preserve intrinsic motivation *if* the player is failing. That is to say, if a player is really intrinsically motivated as an accountant, but he's not good at his job, why would we want to preserve his intrinsic desire? Overjustification generally doesn't negatively affect players with good performance or strong personal motivation, though some extrinsic rewards can readily be seen as manipulative or negative if used in the wrong context.

One obvious conclusion of the intrinsic/extrinsic behavioral questions is that once you start giving someone a reward, you have to keep her in that reward loop forever. This consideration informs the total cost of ownership question for gamification and should be part of your calculations (though you need not budget for it immediately).

Exercise: How Competitive Are You?

Are you a hyper-competitive killer type? Take Houston and Smither's Competitiveness Test to measure how competitive you are at GamificationU.com.

Old Beliefs

In our research on competitiveness, overjustification, and incentives/rewards, we came across a series of old beliefs, many of which were broadly held, that question some of the core tenets of gamification. Here are some of those beliefs, as well as thoughts on placing them in context.

Old belief #1

Intrinsic motivation is better than extrinsic rewards.

Does it even matter? Or more importantly, can an intrinsic motivation be counted on? The crux of the problem is that by sitting around waiting for people's intrinsic drive to become better, to do more, or to help other people, we find that we don't always get the desired results. But when we make the motivation extrinsic, we shift that locus of responsibility from hoping it happens to a structure and process for making it happen.

Gamification works better if and when we can align intrinsic motivations and extrinsic rewards, and we should strive to achieve that wherever possible. But our new belief is that we should accept players and their motivational states as they are, and try to help them get to where they would like to go, as well as where we'd like them to be.

Old belief #2

Intrinsic motivators create greatness, while extrinsic motivators are nothing more than pellets dropped for rats in a cage.

Our fundamental observation is that when something is designed well, it feels intrinsic to the player. He perceived that it was intrinsically driven whether or not it was (just as a good sales person can convince the buyer it was his idea to buy that set of encyclopedias in the first place). Further, a player might not know something was intrinsic to him until he discovered it through an extrinsic motivator.

As designers, we must keep a watchful eye on our players. We have to attempt to know some things about our players and their wants, even if they might not know them yet. A good example is the motivation to lose weight—Americans, by and large (no pun intended), struggle with obesity. Most of them want to be healthier and skinnier. But despite the intrinsic desire, the process is disconnected. A designer, however, would say that what is missing is a well-designed reward and incentive loop for losing weight.

The new belief is that we are helping people, to some extent, reach a higher potential—and to discover things about themselves that they didn't already know.

Old belief #3

The best designs are intrinsic: take, for instance, Priority Boarding.

It may surprise you to know that Continental (now United) Airlines actually invented the model of the priority boarding lines and carpets. Once upon a time, we boarded according to the instructions of a voice over a loud speaker, with first class leading the way, followed by designated seating rows. But United realized that for no more than the cost of a carpet and a sign, they could take what was once a private status benefit and make it public—and desirable.

To be clear, there is no new benefit granted to the people boarding from the red carpet. They always boarded first. They always got the extra overhead bin space and legroom, the drinks before takeoff. In fact, the plane doesn't leave any sooner and the pretzels aren't any better than they were before. The only benefit is a demonstrable one—and the only true beneficiary is United Airlines.

While some flyers show off that they have red-carpet status, the other flyers will wonder, "Why is that guy on the red carpet and how do I get there?"

Today, the red-carpet boarding design feels normal. In fact, it feels intrinsic, like it's always been there. But it hasn't. It works because the system in which it resides is very compelling. It proves that when the gamified experience is good enough, benefits can be created out of thin air. For example, you can even add a baggage fee and then remove it for people with high status in the frequent-flyer game. Even though no one paid a baggage fee three years ago, with a little added friction, it has now become— like the red carpet—a reward.

A good extrinsic motivation is a good map to intrinsic motivation. The better a designer knows his players, resulting in a better game design, the less it will feel to the player like being on a wheel, and the more it will feel like it was her idea to begin with. That's the holy grail of gamification: a game so well designed that the player's actions just feel normal. We believe it can be done in almost any experience.

Progression to Mastery

One well-accepted theory is that players in any experience are seeking mastery. Why do people go to Weight Watchers meetings? It's safe to assume it's probably not for the free coffee, but rather to master their weight and health.

In original research by Dreyfus for the U.S. Army in the 1980s (since revised in the 1990s), a series of stages of mastery emerged when looking at how people engage with systems, as shown in Figure 2-5.

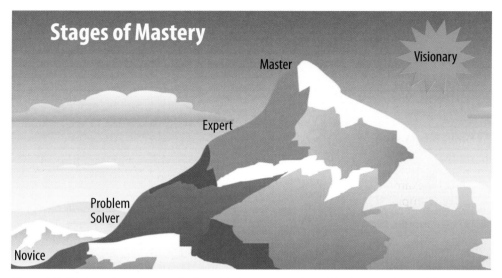

Figure 2-5. Mastery of a system can be thought of as a mountain—rising from novice to visionary across a series of steps..

Dreyfus outlines five core levels:

Novice

A novice is someone who's just arrived to the experience. It is his first minute with a new system. Using the example of a 1040 tax form, the first time someone sees it, he is a total novice to the system. To him, it has little depth of meaning. It's just a form.

Problem solver

Similar to a novice but with some information already in hand, a problem solver is on her way toward figuring out what is going on. On a 1040 tax form, the problem solver has already learned that the instructions are on the back of the form. She may not understand how the numbers are derived or why she is calculating AMT, but she is able to do it—and if she can't, critically, she knows whom to call to find out how.

Expert

An expert has already started to learn how the system works. In other words, an expert user of the 1040 tax form knows he needs all of his W2 forms and 1099s attached to this form. If he doesn't submit all of them, regardless of timing, his tax return may be audited, returned, or recalculated by the IRS. That is not an obvious bit of information. An expert knows to hold on to his tax return until he gets it or he can input the number (and skip attaching the form entirely). At the expert level, a player knows something that is not obvious to the casual player.

Master

> A master believes that she truly understands the system. She believes that she is in control. She is aware of its nuances and its ins and outs. A master is also likely to identify personally or culturally with the system. For example, with a 1040 tax form, the master might be thinking, "I'm an accountant. I've been doing taxes for 25 years. No one knows this process better than me."

Visionary

> A visionary is a special kind of master. He puts himself inside the designer's shoes. A visionary can look at the 1040 form and find a flaw in the calculation on line 17. Most designers have probably experienced the enthusiasm of a visionary, for example, by getting a 3 a.m. email from a customer announcing a great idea to improve some minute aspect of a system.

No player should be obligated or expected to progress to visionary—your system should enable the player to stop at any level. If a player is happy to remain a problem solver, this is a perfectly acceptable level to maintain. In fact, it could be argued that most people, when it comes to the 1040 tax form, remain decidedly at the problem-solver level. If they need to go deeper, they will call an expert (most likely an accountant). In any game system, a player should be able to stop or leave at any time she wants.

Exercise: Rank the Top Five Player Actions on the Scale of Progression to Mastery

Recall your top five player actions and decide where they should go on the scale of progression to mastery—understanding, of course, that not everything can or should come at the novice level. Additionally, while some actions may recur along your progression system (recommend or share, for example might repeat at novice, master, and expert), just focus on the first instance of the verb. Pay close attention to how you reveal complexity. Find a version of the mastery mountain at GamificationU.com that you can use for this exercise.

Socializing actions should happen across all levels of the mastery chain. Recommending can take place at both the novice and expert levels. To some degree, it isn't a bad idea to expose every level to the accomplishments of the others.

For a business built around artistic expression—an art-sharing site, for example—the player at the novice level must be able to view site content easily. At the problem-solver level, he might rate the photos on the site. But as a designer, how can you reveal complexity in a measured way? Most networks of this kind, such as DeviantArt (*www.deviantart.com*) or Etsy (*www.etsy.com*) allow anyone to upload their art from day one in an effort to ensure maximum content. But is that good? What if you want to qualify prospective contributors based on their demonstrable knowledge of how your system works? Perhaps you'd opt to hold back "creation" (or upload) until the expert level in order to maintain the integrity of your site.

Notice that we didn't necessarily advocate for holding back posting ability based on how good the art itself is. That might be better handled with peer feedback/ratings. We might use the players' systemic knowledge as a simple proxy to weed out unqualified newbies. Ultimately, the effect might be entirely the same as a vetting process.

Obviously, uploading/creation can happen at a beginner level, but perhaps curation might be a better beginner action. Though clearly not appropriate in every context, curation *is* a form of creative expression! For the seller audience on eBay, curation crosses all levels of mastery. By procuring positive ratings, the seller gains credibility to players at the novice and problem-solving levels. At the expert and master levels, it allows them to play more competitively—measured by how well they stack up against other sellers. Once a seller reaches thousands/millions of sales within the game, it is just assumed she has become a master or potential visionary.

Designing for the Novice, Considering the Elder

The preceding examples highlight the fact that the game someone is playing at the novice level is different than the game someone else is playing at the expert or master level. The top levels of a game are sometimes called the *elder game*. When beginning a new design, it is important to focus on the nonelder game, the game being played at the novice and problem-solving levels.

This is because, with few exceptions, most people in the world are not yet your customers, which means they are novices and problem solvers in your system. If you begin with a strong and compelling base design, you will find there is no downside to setting aside the elder game until you need it.

Beating the Boss Level

When United Airlines' Mileage Plus frequent-flyer program began in the 1980s, it wasn't conceived that players would ever reach the million-mile flown mark. After all, a million miles is the equivalent of more than 2,000 hours (or a full-time work year) spent in a moving plane, not counting any travel, airport, security, boarding, taxiing, or deplaning time. So, when the first players began reaching that milestone, United pieced together a Million Miler level with lifetime benefits.

At first the level was informal, but it was formalized in the 1990s when United discovered that after those players passed one million miles, they tended to reduce or stop playing altogether. Their best, most loyal players simply leveled out of the game. It was inevitable. Without a continuation of the game, there is no longer an incentive to play. In the case of these Mileage Plus players, they had beaten the "boss level" of the game.

Then, a few years ago, United formalized the two- and three-million-mile tiers for Mileage Plus. In the beginning, it wasn't important for United to have a three-million-mile tier—now it is. Luckily, they had a system in place that was open and flexible enough to keep the game changing and expanding as needed. In mid-2011, the first United flyer to reach ten million miles was announced. His reward: a plane with his name on it and a titanium card.

In another example, *FarmVille* began with 70 levels, but more were created as players began completing the original 70. These examples show that you must not lose sight of the elder game because of its potential and hopeful inevitability. However, you don't need to design for it until it's necessary.

Exercise: Rank Your Own Goals and Objectives for Game Design

As a gamification designer, you should consider the importance of each of the following as you build your system (and feel free to add your own):

- Managing money
- Making and keeping relationships
- Career success
- Helping others and doing "good"
- Being knowledgeable
- Being healthy
- Other

Motivational Moment: Be the Sherpa

On the journey to mastery, it is important to know where your brand, service, product, or concept lives in the ecosystem. You are not the mountain. You are the Sherpa.

Your player is on his own journey. You must make it your goal to help pave and structure that journey. To obtain long-term, enduring loyalty and connection from your players, you must guide them up the mountain. You don't need to be the mountain and you don't need to create it. You simply need to lead them up.

Be their Sherpa. Give them the status, access, power, and tools to get them where they need to go. Do it right and they'll be yours forever.

CHAPTER 3

Game Mechanics:
Designing for Engagement (Part I)

Game design is a relatively new, unaccredited discipline with roots in both psychology and systems-thinking. When creating a gamified experience, we leverage many aspects of game design, while focusing on the core elements that will produce the greatest impact for our players. For example, we generally ignore narrative structure in gamification because we are building "nonfiction" experiences. That is, the arc of your gamified system is based on your player's and your brand's stories—as they already exist.

Luckily, you don't need nor should you want to become a full-fledged game designer. While many reference works (such as the excellent *The Art of Game Design: A Book of Lenses* by Jesse Schell [Morgan Kaufmann]) can help deepen your understanding of how to make games, we've filtered the key elements of the discipline here to focus on the most important. Our view of game design is narrow, but it is highly optimized for gamification.

MDA Framework

One of the most frequently leveraged frameworks of game design is referred to as MDA—which stands for:

- Mechanics
- Dynamics
- Aesthetics

The MDA framework is a postmortem analysis of the elements of a game. It helps us use systems-thinking to describe the interplay of those game elements and apply them outside of games.

Mechanics make up the functioning components of the game. At their core, they allow a designer ultimate control over the levers of the game, giving her the ability to guide player actions. *Dynamics*, meanwhile, are the player's interactions with those mechanics. They determine what each player is doing in response to the mechanics of the system, both individually and with other players. Sometimes, game mechanics and game dynamics are used interchangeably, but they are markedly different.

Finally, the *aesthetics* of the system are how the game makes the player feel during interaction. Game aesthetics can be viewed as the composite outcome of the mechanics and dynamics as they interact with and create emotions.

Game Mechanics

The mechanics of a gamified system are made up of a series of tools that, when used correctly, promise to yield a meaningful response (aesthetics) from the players. For our purposes, we'll focus on seven primary elements: points, levels, leaderboards, badges, challenges/quests, onboarding, and engagement loops. In this chapter, we'll cover the first three of these mechanics, starting with the heart of any gaming system—points. See Chapter 4 for information on the remaining elements.

Points

Points are important regardless of whether their accumulation is shared among players, or even between the designer and the player. When you first consider a point system, you might immediately think of a goal in a sporting event, redeemable points in a video game, or bonus points awarded to players for successfully completing special tasks within a game.

No matter what your preconception of points may be, they are an absolute requirement for all gamified systems. As the designer, it is imperative that you value and track every move your players make—even if those scores are only visible to you in your management console and not to them. In this way, you can see how your players are interacting with your system, design for outcomes, and make appropriate adjustments.

Point systems run the gamut from in-your-face obvious to barely visible, and they serve a wide range of purposes. As such, there are a few types we'd like to point out that you've doubtless encountered in your life.

Real-World Point Examples

There are many types of scorekeeping you may already be familiar with.

Cash score

This number indicates how much money you have in the bank. Considering how much we value money in our society, it's curious that we don't just tell others our bank balance in casual conversation. Instead of breaking this social taboo, we give cues on our cash scores through what we wear, where we go on vacation, what cars we drive, etc. Instead of shouting out our actual score, we signal it using status objects. In this point model, signals tell the score, exact numbers don't.

Video game score

A much more overt score is that in almost any video game. The score is always at the corner of the screen, letting the player know how close or far he is from the next level, other players, and ultimately winning the game. Few systems in real life keep the score as omnipresent as video games.

Social networking score

When Facebook was developed, there was nothing overtly indicating that the number of friends a user had served much function whatsoever. Similarly, the number of followers or mentions on Twitter was never explicitly pointed to as a designated "score." But they are. Most players can name how many friends and followers they have on any given social network. What's more, they can probably name who among their friends has an unusually high number of friends or followers. An inventory of sorts is taken, simply because Facebook and Twitter place the "score" prominently on the page. Moreover, social network scores have profoundly affected the fortunes of at least one major social network: Orkut.

Google Orkut was an eponymous social networking site created by a Google employee. Most social network users may not have heard of it, but there is at least one place in the world where Orkut is the #1 social networking site: Brazil.

While designing the site, Google put in place a simple leaderboard listing the number of people per country who had signed up for Orkut. When Brazil entered the top group on that leaderboard, something unexpected started to happen—Brazilians began to host spontaneous Orkut sign-up parties. The goal was to overtake the number one spot held by the United States. Thus, Orkut became Brazil's #1 social networking site—handily besting Facebook—all because of a score and an innocuous leaderboard.

Composite metrics

Any metric has the power to become a type of score. Sometimes it is better to create a composite metric in order to convey complex data in a simple form. A FICO score, for example, is an amalgam of a whole series of different pieces of information—from average monthly credit card payments to amassed debt over a lifetime. We could, of course, show different scores for each vector we wanted to measure. But by summarizing the complexity of creditworthiness into a single number, anyone from a prospective landlord to a bank clerk can derive meaning from it without needing a Ph.D. in economics.

Similarly, Weight Watchers creates a metric that calls on a series of numbers—from body mass index to weight to daily calorie intake—in order to follow the progress of their users who are seeking a healthier lifestyle. In the same vein, Klout—a web service that offers a social media influence score—tells you and others how you rank in influence and importance on Twitter. It doesn't take into account just a single vector, but rather a series of numbers that are amalgamated into one.

Point Systems

In gamification, we can leverage one of five point designs to form the foundation of our experience. In some cases, your point system will be overt, direct, and highly motivational. In some designs, you might use four different kinds of points to achieve your objectives. In still other instances, points will take a back seat to other mechanics, doing their duties in the background as the designer's workhorse.

Whatever you end up choosing, you'll need to get a good handle on point system basics and options. Your points palette includes the following:

- Experience points
- Redeemable points
- Skill points
- Karma points
- Reputation points

Experience points

Of the five kinds of point systems, the most important are experience points (XP). Unlike airline miles, XP do not serve as any type of currency within the system. They are how you watch, rank, and guide your player.

Everything a player does within the system will earn her XP—and, in general, XP never goes down and cannot be redeemed. By assigning XP to every activity in the system, the designer aligns his behavioral objectives with the player in a long-term way. In some systems, XP can expire—say monthly or annually—to create goal loops. This pattern can be observed in the requalification periods used in frequent-flyer programs—and expiry can serve the important purpose of "resetting" the game to level the playing field.

However, perhaps even more importantly, XP never maxes out. A player continues to earn them as long as she plays the game. That is the power of XP.

Redeemable points

The second point system is made up of redeemable points (RP). Unlike XP, RP can fluctuate. The expectation for most people is that these points are usable within the system in exchange for things. They are earned and cashed, similar to the frequent-flyer miles we redeem for awards. The term for this loop in social games and loyalty programs is "earn and burn," which clearly indicates the purpose of an RP system.

RPs generally form the foundation of a virtual economy, and are often given names like coins, bucks, cash, etc. Like any economy, you will need to monitor, manage, and tweak the flows of capital to ensure everything runs smoothly, as well as to avoid massive inflation or deflation. In addition, redeemable points come with substantial issues from a legal and regulatory standpoint.

 Note. *For more on the legal issues in redeemable point systems, visit GamificationU.com and complete the challenges.*

Skill points

The third point system is called a skill point system. Skill points are assigned to specific activities within the game and are tangential to both XP and RP. They are a bonus set of points that allow a player to gain experience/reward for activities along-side the core.

By assigning skill points to an activity, we direct the player to complete some key alternate tasks and subgoals. Classic examples of skill points are found in *Dungeons & Dragons* and other similar games where you have skills, such as magic and power, and each has a different score. In the nongame context, you might assign a set of varied skill points on a photo-sharing website. For example, players may earn some points for the quality of their photos and other points for the quality of comments (although this is rare in gamification, depending on the circumstances, it might be worthwhile to keep them separate).

Karma points

Karma points are a unique system that rarely appear in classic games. The sole purpose of karma is to give points away. That is, players gain no benefit from keeping their karma points, only from sharing them. Often, karma points are given as part of a regular grind, or check in behavior, for example: earn 3 karma points for every monthly check in.

The main purpose of karma points in your design is to create a behavioral path for altruism and user reward. For example, if you want users to thank each other for a job well done in a challenge, instead of issuing virtual currency or gifts, you can let them give each other karma. This will preserve the altruistic feeling of the interaction while minimizing the tendency to game the system.

UserVoice is a good example of this system. Using karma points, players vote for and against potential features they'd like to see built. If the player's vote wins and those features are built, he gets karma points back to allocate to new activities, and so forth. The only purpose of karma points in the UserVoice model is to give them away.

Reputation points

Finally, reputation points make up the most complex point system. Any time a system requires trust between two or more parties that you can't explicitly guarantee or manage, a reputation system is key. Its purpose is to act as a proxy for trust.

The reason why reputation systems are generally more complex lies both in how they are designed and how they are used. In general, they must incorporate a wide range of activities in order to be meaningful—and the design must consider incentives and unintended consequences. Moreover, because they are a proxy for trust, players will certainly attempt to game the system. Integrity and consistency will be paramount.

How to Use Point Systems

To begin with, it's imperative to string an XP architecture around your gamified system. It informs you and your players about which activities are more important.

Redeemable points, on the other hand, should be used when you want to create a virtual economy. Virtual economies are most valuable when you are looking to incentivize broad behaviors, large communities, and/or leverage economics to drive behavior. However, they also have unique challenges, such as legal and regulatory issues that are complex and rapidly changing.

Another challenge of redeemable points is how they are perceived. If you announce a great redeemable point system, the first thing players will do is see what they can get. If what is offered feels neither meaningful nor realistic, you might lose the players entirely. In other words, if a player looks at the redemption opportunity and thinks, "Yeah right. I'm not going to win a free car for watching a video," then that player might not believe it is worth his while to stay within the system. Similarly, another might see that she could obtain free pizza for her points, but she happens to not like pizza. In both those cases, you might be at risk for losing players.

Reputation points are complex but often necessary in a system. The biggest problem with them, however, is that they are easy to "game". TripAdvisor is a website that shares customer reviews about travel worldwide. The site is so successful that it is reportedly responsible for 30% of all hotel bookings. Therefore, hotels have a vested interest in not only seeing that they are favorably reviewed, but also that other hotels are not. Although no official statistics exist, a cursory review of TripAdvisor will immediately reveal a host of obviously "chaff" reviews.

Yelp—a site that allows users to review local restaurants and entertainment venues—runs into a similar set of problems. To date, the only real way to determine which reviews are real and which are gamed is to read a lot of them. Neither of these sites has implemented a reputation system that is scaled to the level of complexity or value that's actually being created. By comparison, eBay has long held that its fully featured reputation point system, as shown in Figure 3-1, is a core asset that facilitates trust and transaction volume.

Figure 3-1. eBay's reputation point system is more sophisticated than most and reflects the need for trust between parties.

Virtual economies

The power of a virtual economy is that it allows a designer to bring in a lot of money and control how it goes out. Any macroeconomics major might recall a few communist and socialist countries that have operated under that very premise. In Cuba, a traveler can exchange any currency for a convertible Cuban peso, but it can be nearly impossible to change that peso back to its original bills.

That's how most economies are designed in the virtual world as well. For example, Zynga's *FarmVille* has a completely one-way exchange system. A player can only put money in, and since there are no real-world rewards to redeem for, it all stays in the game.

In 2010, Zynga launched a well-known promotion with 7-Eleven and Slurpee. Logically, you might think that a player could exchange *FarmVille* credits to pay for a Slurpee in the store. However, the promotion was that for every Slurpee purchased, a player got bonus *FarmVille* credits. The value of the virtual economy, in this case, was greater than that of the real-world reward.

Virtual economies and secondary markets

Secondary markets—where users can buy and sell currency or objects offsite from the game—have been, by and large, a bane to the designers of the MMOGs from which they emerged. They were frequently tolerated as a community feature because the designers hadn't taken them into consideration in the first place. However, in new gamified designs, the options for secondary markets are often greatly reduced. Today's designers seek to control as many aspects of the virtual economy as possible—and secondary markets oppose that objective.

Currency Denominations

The perceived value of virtual currency can be closely tied to the currency that players are actually using. For example, the equivalent of $1 U.S. is 1,000 Korean Won (they both buy approximately a soft drink from a street vendor). So, when denominating a virtual currency for Korea, it's worthwhile to offer 1,000 times more currency per unit than in the United States. New social games automatically renumber all player views based on the player's country of origin, denominating everything in U.S. dollars behind the scenes. The parallels to the real-world economy are not incidental.

Dual economy

A well-functioning virtual economy will control player demand with minimum complexity. It even allows for a certain level of fluidity in game play. If a designer creates a promotion without the help of a virtual economy, new and cumbersome explanations must be disclosed each time. For example, "Tell three friends about us and get a scratch-off card that gets you 20% off a t-shirt," or "Tell four friends, and we'll throw in a basketball," etc.

But in a virtual economy, nothing more needs to be done than to tell the player, "Tell three friends and get 200 points." This promotion needs no explanation—the player already knows what that will get him. Therefore, marketing is optimized.

In fact, *FarmVille* demonstrates this very well in what is called a dual economy. It has created two currencies within the system of the game: cash and coins (conveniently, U.S. dollars convert into both). Each is used for different kinds of items within the game, as shown in Figure 3-2.

Notice also in Figure 3-2 that the U.S. dollar-*FarmVille* currency conversion ratio varies based on the amount invested. This sliding-scale conversion rate not only makes it more attractive for users to invest more cash up front, it creates additional confusion by using complex fractions in conversion and uneven numbers on the converted unit (e.g., 70,600 or 650).

Figure 3-2. FarmVille's dual economy: cash for special items, coins for everything else. Both convert from U.S. dollars. Note the complex conversion rates, which obfuscate convertibility for users.

The benefits of a dual currency are manifold. For example, a dual currency can enable you to set wildly different values on items within the economy while also controlling the inbound monetary supply. This means that you can more easily vary the values for different activities without having to inflate/deflate everything at the same time. While this technique is not for every gamified experience, it can be useful if your community is large enough (and your virtual economy is dynamic enough).

Exercise: Assigned Point Values

In this exercise, pull out the top player actions you defined in Chapter 2, and assign a point value to them. Begin by choosing the lightest-weight action and giving it a value of 100. Now, what are the other actions worth to you?

When doing this exercise, don't consider how the points will be used or whether they are re- deemable. Instead, think about the relative value of each one of these actions. Based on your businesses' goals and objectives, which is worth more and by what percent?

Keep in mind that in major social games there is a funnel. For example, for every 100 people that "like" something, 10 of them convert; and for every 10 conversions, a business earns $30. So, every "like" is worth 30 cents. Even though value is fluid, and you'll only begin to understand it once it is put into action, in the beginning, you must stake out a point value for every action in play.

Example: Assigned Point Values

Perhaps the top five social actions you chose in Chapter 2 were Explore, Comment, Join, Recommend, and Express. And in the above exercise, you assigned them the following values:

Action	Point value
Explore	100 points
Comment	200 points
Join	400 points
Express	400 points
Recommend	200 points

You might reason that exploring the site is the least beneficial of the five actions to the objectives of the company, even if it is important to the gamified experience of the player. Therefore, you assign "Explore" the smallest value. A comment, on the other hand, is worth double since it might lend quite a bit of value to your commu- nity at large.

In general, joining is an often underappreciated action. However, it is quite a hurdle to get players to sign up for your system. So, giving "Join" four times the weight afforded "Explore" is actually the right idea. There is great value in having a player's email address and name—not to mention the new level of value she has attached to your system when she joins. Lastly, "Join" is a once-only action, so it's likely to be much more valuable.

By weighting "Express" as four times more valuable than "Explore," you are making the statement that the social benefits of a player proselytizing on behalf of your system is a deeply important action—and perhaps even fundamental to your system. Obviously, "Recommend" is among the most extreme forms of player viral expression, so it is naturally weighted more heavily.

Some actions require us to think about curbing point earnings. For example, if comment is worth 200 points ad infinitum, users would clearly be incentivized to post a ton of comments. What we should consider is slowing down the XP earnings over time, without making the experience less fun. For example, we might make the first comment worth 200, the next 3 worth 150, and the rest worth only 50. The exact ratios are up to you, but some brakes on earning XP (or RP) are usually essential.

Levels

In most games, levels indicate progress—though they are not as exclusive in this role as they once were. For example, in the arcade game *Ms. Pac-Man*, levels are clearly expressed by the color of the ghosts, the layout of the maze, and the kind of fruit that loops around the maze. Of course, designers of gamified experiences aren't going to use traditional levels like those found in video games, but understanding them can add a powerful tool to your design. Levels serve as a marker for players to know where they stand in a gaming experience over time.

Level Design

In *Ms. Pac-Man*, a player knows instantly that the level has changed because, in addition to being told directly and seeing diferent colors, the game has become more difficult and the prizes for rewarded behaviors increase in value. Meanwhile, though the Ms. Pac-Man avatar moves at the same pace, the ghosts move faster, and the safety time zone delineations are shorter.

In game design, level difficulty is not linear. In other words, it does not take 100 points to get to level one, 200 for level two, 300 for level three, and so on. Instead, difficulty increases in a curvilinear form. In *Ms. Pac-Man*, an expert player knows that after level three, the ghosts slow down again and the safety time zone delineations increase. The screen might continue to harbor more complexities, but like most level design, difficulty increases exponentially through each level and then decreases over time; an example of this is shown in Figure 3-3.

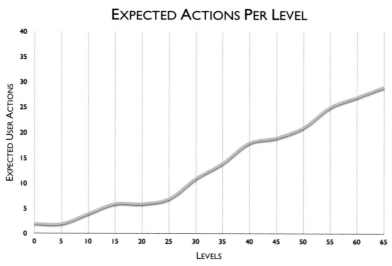

Figure 3-3. Level complexity. Although this progression is different in every game, the basic concept shows that progression through levels is not linear or exponential.

In the game *Angry Birds,* the complexity transitions from one level to the next have proven extremely engaging. Using well-designed levels, the player progresses almost seamlessly, gaining confidence and experience. However, at one of the much higher levels in the game—level 21 in the first board, for example—the player encounters a decidedly more complicated sequence of challenges than the one before it. It is, in fact, so difficult that there is only one sequence of actions that will get the player through. It is the first time in the game that a player is likely to notice that he has passed to a new and more difficult level.

Some might consider this move by the designers of *Angry Birds* controversial. Inevitably, players who find the challenge too much will drop out of the game. But on the other side of the argument, those who pass the level are more likely to feel as though they've achieved something special and have become part of an exclusive group. Clearing the level will unlock the next board, so it's a major achievement (and one that bedeviled your authors for quite a while).

Progression of difficulty

The average length of the Nintendo arcade game *Donkey Kong* lasts less than one minute. This is because the first level of *Donkey Kong* is incredibly hard. Realistically, an arcade in the 1980s would have a vested interest in their players losing faster, thereby inserting additional quarters sooner.

In today's gaming systems, we are interested in longer, stickier games. So, today's designs start at the very simplest levels and move progressively toward the complex.

In PopCap's iPhone game *Plants vs. Zombies*, a player moves from one level to the next with the difficulty of the game increasing with each new level. A quick look at the game's first and twentieth boards (shown in Figure 3-4) illustrates just how much more difficult the game becomes as the player progresses. The board grows visibly crowded with characters and obstacles.

Figure 3-4. In PopCap's Plants vs. Zombies, the progression of level complexity from the first level (left) to levels 20 and higher (right) is substantial.

In some systems, levels might define the difficulty or the leading element of the game, or else they might serve as a passive marker to give more depth and complexity to your system.

Either way, the best design tips for levels are to make them logical (or easy for the player to understand), extensible (so that you can add levels as needed beyond the initial "boss level"), and flexible. Finally, the levels should be testable and refinable. Level balancing is just as complex as building the game in the first place, and should be tested and retested even as the players are in the game.

Enduring leveling systems

American Express has built an impressive level system using the demonstrability of the credit card itself. Most Americans could probably guess what you were talking about if you simply named off the colors of the AmEx rainbow of credit cards: Green, Gold, Platinum, and Black.

What is interesting about that list is that while green, gold, and platinum all connote money and precious metals, making black the most elite card seems to be a surprising choice. By valuing black as their top tier, American Express changed the color's meaning. Now, black as a top tier is as common as gold and platinum.

Precious Metals

How do we know gold is more valuable than silver and bronze? Unless you regularly monitor the precious metals market, odds are you were taught that fact by other leveling systems in your life, such as the Olympics, which makes use of precious metals in their award system. And because markets aren't truly rational, it's hard to say how much the Olympics rankings affect the price of gold and silver today.

University levels are similarly stamped with a clear ranking both within the confines of the institutions and for the population at large. The degrees bachelor's, master's, and Ph.D. (or doctorate) clearly indicate which level has been achieved. The military and the Boy Scouts have arguably two of the most perfected leveling systems of any institution. From badges and medals, to titles like General and Eagle Scout, even the uniforms indicate who resides where in the levels of the "game." See the sidebar "Boy Scouts and the Military" in Chapter 4 for more information.

Progress bar

Progress bars are appearing all over the Internet. In most incarnations, they use percentages to inform a player of how close she is to completing, for example, all the necessary sign-up information (see Figure 3-5). Principally, they are used to encourage new players to add personal information to a site or to create a deeper core experience. Progress bars work hand in hand with levels, serving as a percentage-based progress guide for a player.

 Note. *The best progress bars never reach 100%.*

Consider the Linkedin progress bar (Figure 3-5) for a moment. While it is a powerful and broadly known example of progress mechanics, it also has two major flaws. First, that it reaches 100%: the best progress bars continue to be viable well beyond 100. Second, that you have to complete the steps in order to progress reflects the lack of a good XP system at Linkedin.

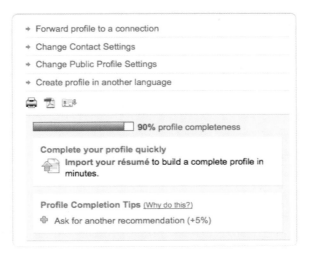

Figure 3-5. Example progress bar on LinkedIn.

Example: Using a Metaphor

Say you are developing a gamified experience for a company that sells women's shoes. You decide that it makes sense to title your levels based on candy to invoke both playfulness and color. These are the names you choose from the lowest level to the highest: peppermint, cherry cordial, marshmallow, chocolate, and truffle.

Using a Metaphor

Like American Express or the Boy Scouts, creatively describe the proposed levels for your gamified experience. Without using precious metals or gems, imagine what an interesting leveling system for your product would be like.

While these levels certainly sound like they would appeal to your demographic, the problem with a metaphorical system is that people can lose track of where they are by confusing, for example, chocolate with truffle. Another thing to avoid is accruing a list of levels that come off as "cutesy"—that is, unless cute is in the honest voice of your player.

Finding Your Voice

One experience relayed from a prospective client was telling. The client made a type of financial marketplace software connecting investors and deals. They had assigned a value to animals like bulls, bears, sharks, whales and pigs—all common terms in the finance industry. So when developing a gamified experience for that demographic, they used those animals in the leveling system. Imagine attempting to engage a 50-year-old investment banker with an adorable pig avatar; it's probably not going to work. But that's exactly what they did—to deleterious effect. Suffice to say that they had to remove the too-cute-for-words characters and replace them with something more sophisticated.

Although a designer might be drawn to using words that relate to a specific community—as in the case of a bull, a bear, and a pig, or even in the case of those chocolates and peppermints—perhaps the level should not be represented by a literal or cartoon representation. Perhaps it would be more effective to use a color to represent the image, or even a depiction of the word itself. It all depends on your audience, so you must know your players.

Leaderboards

The purpose of a leaderboard is to make simple comparisons. Unsurprisingly, most people don't need any explanation when they encounter a leaderboard. By default, we see an ordered list with a score beside each name, and we understand that we are looking at a ranking system.

In any '80s arcade, a novice who might approach a *Galaga* or *Moon Patrol* cabinet would find on the screen a list of high scorers—most of which trailed enough zeros to render a potential player dumbfounded. Talk about a terrible disincentive to play the game! Even when the number scale is completely meaningless or opaque, the player still feels that four million points is a lot, so it's probably difficult to attain (unless it's 4,000,000 Vietnamese Dong, the equivalent of about $200 U.S. dollars at press time—see the sidebar "Currency Denominations" earlier in this chapter).

Leaderboard Types

There are two kinds of leaderboards largely used today.

The no-disincentive leaderboard

The leaderboard of today has seen some radical redesign since the heyday of pinball machines and quarter arcades. In the era of Facebook and the social graph, leaderboards are mostly tools for creating social incentive, rather than disincentive.

They accomplish this simply by taking the player and putting him right in the middle. It doesn't matter where he falls in ranking order—whether he is #81 or #200,000—the player will see himself right in the middle of the leaderboard. Below him, he will see friends who are on his tail, and above him he will see exactly how close he is to the next best score. And he will know exactly what he has to do to beat it.

However, if the player is actually in the top 10 or top 20, the leaderboard should reflect this directly. In the case of these players, the leaderboard should show them their literal ranking, which is likely to be meaningful to them.

The infinite leaderboard

In an arcade, there are not too many ways to allow every player to exist on a given game's leaderboard forever. At some point, a player's score will be beaten and she will fall off—or she will hit a number and sit there for weeks until someone finally beats it. In today's world, there are ways to control leaderboards such that no player ever falls off or gets stuck.

Doodle Jump, a popular iPhone game, allows its players to see the leaderboard sliced in various ways: locally, socially, and globally (see Figure 3-6). A local view shows a player where he ranks compared to others in the system in his immediate area. Socially, he can see how he ranks among his friends and followers in the game. A global view allows the same thing within the system as a whole.

There is no reason players can't slice and dice their leaderboard however they want. In fact, tracking the leaderboard behavior of a player will also inform the designer about her players. For example, a player with a deep interest in leaderboard positioning is likely to be a more competitive player and can be guided accordingly.

Leaderboards can also be displayed with a limited available view for the player, which can be an important tool in a game with millions of players. *Flight Control*—the air traffic control game mentioned in Chapter 1 and shown in Figure 1-1—has a leaderboard that displays other players at the same level, ranked by proximity and recency to you. This kind of multilayered leaderboard helps to manage a game with millions of players.

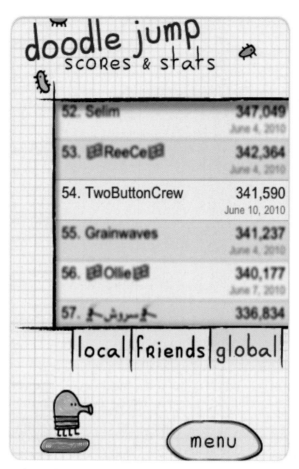

Figure 3-6. Doodle Jump's simple but multidimensional leaderboard allows for flexible views of progress and comparison.

Other popular social leaderboards include Klout, which, for example, ranked fans of the Sacramento Kings basketball team by their Klout score—showing users' social power on Twitter. Also, Yelp's mobile app ranks a user's top weekly check-ins. The leaderboard can be cut by friends or by royalty—the high scorers in the game, similar to mayors in Foursquare. Additionally, Yelp cleverly defaults to the weekly view of success, ensuring that the leaderboard data is fresher and more dynamic for players.

Privacy and Leaderboards

Sometimes creating a leaderboard isn't as obvious as it seems. In the event that the items being compared are sensitive or difficult to quantify, leaderboards present a unique challenge. Since the role of the leaderboard is to publicly compare, how does one compare information best kept private?

For example, a gym has a vested interest in helping its users achieve more healthful lifestyles or meet their fitness goals. Therefore, asking a novice to walk in, step on a scale, and have his weight compared with other gym members is probably going to lose that gym quite a few prospective members. Not only is sharing a person's weight publicly a potentially shame-inducing experience, not everyone joining the gym is there to lose weight. Some people join to train for a marathon, relax in the sauna, or even gain muscle weight.

It might become clear that more than one leaderboard is necessary to meet the goals of the gym. For a novice player, a leaderboard that lists her attendance might be a great introduction to the system. Runners might want to be part of a leaderboard where they race other gym members. And while body builders might even want to share their weight and watch their numbers increase publicly, people seeking to lose weight might be less inclined to play if public humiliation is part of the game. Furthermore, there is the potential that any of these leaderboards might induce unhealthy results if players push themselves to win.

Creating leaderboards using sensitive or private information is challenging but not impossible. Abstracted point systems can ensure that each player maintains a program that is healthful for them while sizing up their accomplishments in a public leaderboard. Ultimately, designers will have to keep their goals in mind and maintain an awareness of their overall objectives—and take some responsibility for the leaderboard's power.

 Note. *Visit* http://GamificationU.com *to find out more about leaderboards, access supplemental content, and download the exercises that go with this chapter.*

With the truly competitive, a straight leaderboard can be a powerful tool for motivation. But for most explorers and socializers, and for many achievers, it can be both positive and negative. Consider your players' motivations and make your leaderboard social: it's a win-win proposition.

CHAPTER 4

Game Mechanics:
Designing for Engagement (Part II)

Badges

Although it's easy to forget, Foursquare did not invent badges. They've been around for a long time and are distinctively omnipresent in our world. On the back of most cars, a small string of numbers, letters, and a logo tell everyone on the road a lot about both the vehicle and its driver. The automotive industry calls that a badge, and it signals what kind of engine is under the hood, what kind of price tag was on the car at the dealership, and, therefore, what kind of driver is behind the wheel. Carmakers prominently display those badges knowing full well that car owners take them very seriously.

In addition to signaling status, people desire badges for all kinds of reasons. For many people, collecting is a powerful drive. Other players enjoy the sudden rush of surprise or pleasure when an unexpected badge shows up in a gamified system. A well-designed, visually valuable badge can also be compelling for purely aesthetic reasons.

For game designers, badges are an excellent way to encourage social promotion of their products and services. Badges also mark the completion of goals and the steady progress of play within the system.

Boy Scouts and the Military

Two of the most enduring badging systems ever developed are those of the Boy Scouts and the military.

In the Boy Scouts, badges serve as a visual point system. If a scout collects a certain number of badges, he is automatically elevated to the next level. In the military, badges are a public display of accomplishment. In both cases, they serve as a reward for the completion of an action that the institution deems important and worthy.

The power of badges to motivate in the military and scouts is so powerful that the core systems have remained intact for hundreds of years. Have you ever participated in a comparably engaging badge system?

Effective and Controversial Badging

In some designs, badges can replace levels as effective progress markers. For example, Foursquare uses check-in counting badges to demarcate levels in lieu of a separate leveling system. As a result of the social, collectible, and visual nature of badges, an increasing number of gamified systems are following in Foursquare's lead.

On the other hand, a concept we call "badgenfreude" suggests that an endless parade of boring and pointless badges have rendered all badges vapid at best and patronizing at worst, leaving many of us believing that badges suck.

However, just because a designer hasn't seen well-executed badging systems doesn't mean they don't exist. And to be clear, Foursquare isn't the only badging system in the virtual world with some level of credibility. But since it is a success story in a place where "badgenfreude" is the norm, for our purposes, let's look at where it succeeds.

Foursquare principally uses badges to represent players' progress and to create for them a sense of delight or surprise. (Figure 4-1 shows a sampling of Foursquare badges.) One of the most interesting things about its system is that it doles out those badges with seeming randomness. How and when Foursquare will badge its players is not always transparent, so players usually don't know what badge comes next. This decision is controversial because the lack of specific goals might frustrate a more competitive player. However, Foursquare's strength is in actualizing pleasant surprises by catching its players off guard with badges.

However, when Foursquare introduced the "Douchebag badge," players had a tremendously split reaction to it. If you checked in to locations tagged as being popular
with a certain kind of clientele, you'd earn this badge. Initially, as it was impossible to
know where these locations were, almost all of the badges were earned unexpectedly.
And while some people loved it and others didn't, this badge clearly invoked the
"voice" and spirit of Foursquare.

*Figure 4-1. Foursquare's badge room is about progress, check-ins across various axes (time and space),
and some indication of future possibility.*

In *FarmVille*, ribbons serve as the badging system (see Figure 4-2). However, unlike
the badges in Foursquare, these ribbons have different tiers for each badging objective, and they act in close concert with challenges. For example, a player can earn
four ribbons, given at various levels of social promotion, for being a good Samaritan.
In effect, she can earn the same badge four times with increasing degrees of achievement. So, while this system is decidedly more complicated than Foursquare's "check
in to win" system, it also reveals the challenges more clearly to the player. In this way,
the player knows what she must do to progress in the game.

Figure 4-2. FarmVille's ribbons are a badging system that combines predictable challenges with achievements.

Combining Surprise with Predictability

In most cases, designers find that a good balance between Foursquare's surprise badges and *FarmVille's* predictable ones will meet the psychological objectives of players. But don't forget collecting and visual appeal!

Badge Examples: The Good, the Bad, and the Ugly

The Huffington Post (*http://www.huffingtonpost.com/*) is a good example of a poor badging system. For one, the proposed badges don't do much to convey the intended progress to mastery. Nor do they offer much in the way of visual value. They also lack a topical or social angle. Fundamentally, it just doesn't seem to be a very compelling system—it's more like a throwaway or afterthought. HuffPo has likely seen small improvements with minimal effort, but as with most gamification, there is much more that could be done.

GetGlue (*http://getglue.com*), on the other hand, badges players for promoting media products socially. Therefore, most of its products come with their own badge system; for example, hit TV shows—such as *Glee*, *Modern Family*, and *The Office*—have their own badging subset. Instead of merely badging for all TV consumption alone, GetGlue badges players for each individual product, as well as their overall progress.

Similarly, GetGlue had a recent promotion surrounding the rebirth of the television classic, *Dr. Who*. The site offered a limited-edition badge for people who checked in for the first six episodes of the new series while it aired in real time. For anyone who is not a fan of the show, this promotion gives very little incentive. But if you are a fan, what could be more compelling than a limited-edition badge designed for a show you love? GetGlue successfully leveraged scarcity and socialization to create great badges.

Exercise: Badge Design

Challenge yourself to design your own badge. What does a badge look like with regard to your products or services?

Keep in mind that consumers respond to good design, collectability, and scarcity.

Download the simple badge design template at GamificationU.com and use it to construct your ideal badge.

Onboarding

Onboarding is the act of bringing a novice into your system. It is a carefully calculated way of thinking about how someone goes from zero to five miles per hour without crashing his car. Although there is a standard web design way of looking at onboarding (throw a huge number of options at a player to make sure he does something, anything) the game view is very, very different.

Lessons from the casual games market have shown that the first minute a player engages with a system are the most important, because that's when most of a player's decisions are made. Just as Malcolm Gladwell describes in *Blink* (Back Bay Books), we are trained to "thin-slice" all kinds of situations and people. Our animal brains are wired to make snap decisions about friend or foe, and then ask questions later. Casual and social game designers understand this incredibly well. They think about players entering a funnel, so they aim to maximize the value and effect of that first minute. Train and engage, but don't overwhelm.

The Order of a Player's First Minute

The first minute a player spends with your system is not the time to explain anything. Instead, allow the player to experience the site. For example, the first time a player arrives at the dating site HOT or NOT (*http://hotornot.com*), she is asked to rate an attractive person through a simple scale of hotness—is this person hot or not? Immediately, the player is experiencing the core behavior of the site and, with that first interaction, she is drawn in.

A fundamental mistake of many systems is to ask a player to register before allowing him to experience the site. For the player, there is nothing to compel him to want to give out personal information to a service he doesn't yet know. The designer's agenda to get the player's valuable information and data might seem overt and off-putting to him.

So, the second thing a good system will offer in that very first minute is something of value. In the case of HOT or NOT, the player is offered the opportunity to view and rank more attractive people. Other sites might offer prizes, achievements (like badges), or virtual items. No matter what the offer is, it should have value for the player.

Then, and only then, ask her to register. Note that the one exception to this rule might be apps that are running inside Facebook where granting permissions is the first required step.

TMI: Too Much Information

It never fails to amaze us when a website thinks it can throw a novice right into the expert level of a game. Also offensive are sites that attempt to mask this flaw by putting up a messy page trying to explain the game in eight paragraphs or less. People online are busy. They have better things to do than read about a game they don't yet care about.

But sites continue to make this mistake. Gowalla (*http://gowalla.com*), for example, begins with a long and complicated written introduction instead of letting players experience the core check-in loop itself. Why does it do this? Facilitating a more interactive first experience, along with the rewards that are so carefully built into it, would definitely serve Gowalla better.

The truth is, almost nobody reads that booklet that comes with every new Monopoly board game (let alone most household appliances or cars). If the game isn't taught by someone who already knows how to play it (a speech that nearly always finishes with, "just play…you'll figure it out"), one person in the group is likely to skim the instructions and share the abridged version with the other players.

So, on a site like Google AdWords (which in its current incarnation has arguably one of the worst designs for novice users), expecting a player to spend time parsing out all of those words, numbers, and complex subheadings is just absurd. A site like that is designed for failure because there is no way for a first time user to win. Yet still, these sites have the gall to ask anyone who comes along to create an ad, pay money, and wait for it to drive traffic to their products and services.

Obviously, Google has had tremendous success with AdWords, but the experience is a turn off that definitely depresses revenue. Novices generally fail because they lack comparisons to gauge performance and are given too many choices. ("The Google content network? What's that?") To their credit, Google is aware of the issue and is actively working to improve it.

Make Winners

Do not set up your novice player to fail on his first interaction with your game. *FrontierVille* offers a very simple approach—their very first screen features a cartoon character introducing himself:

> *"Howdy! They call me Frontier Jack," he says. "Let's start by digging up the grass with the yellow arrow pointin' at it!"*

The image on the screen, as seen in Figure 4-3, shows Frontier Jack, a yellow arrow, and a patch of grass. No one can mess this up. All a player has to do is click just below the yellow arrow.

Figure 4-3. FrontierVille's onboarding process is simple, slowly reveals complexity, and has no option to fail.

At the tutorial level (level zero), there should be no choices. A player should be offered an action at which he cannot fail. Then, he should be rewarded for successfully completing that action. (Even a "Well done!" or a hearty, "I agree," places your player squarely in a very seductive positive-reinforcement loop.) This model, pioneered by social and casual games, has powerful implications for any kind of business, especially a gamified one.

In a nutshell, you want to offer players a clear path that follows this basic pattern:

Action

Reward

Action

Action

Reward

Join (register)

Invite friends

The stages can vary, as can the interval between them, but the basic pattern is enduring. Begin simply by asking players to take a no-risk action. Follow that with a reward and continue the loop, slowly revealing the added complexity of your system, while also training players on how to achieve. It's even better if you can learn something about the player from her behavior without having to explicitly ask her for information.

Guiding Player Experience

Netflix offers an interesting model. While we would argue that it mistakenly asks its users to register immediately, once a user joins, he is hit with a series of meaningful questions that allow the system to get to know him. Using multiple-choice questions, the site instantly organizes the user's experience. By listing movies and asking which he prefers, Netfix gleans all kinds of important data about the player.

Asking the player meaningful questions truly informs his ongoing engagement. If your system is going to show players something they didn't know before, especially using some type of artificial intelligence, a training game can be most useful. Begin training your player by allowing him to engage in the core experience of the site. Next, offer him a reward. Then, slowly begin revealing the complexity of the game.

Remember: A player can't lose at Netflix or at HOT or NOT. Every player wins.

Exercise: Design an A versus B Quiz

Like those used in Netflix or at HOT or NOT, ask your canonical player a question as part of the onboarding experience. Allow the question to be fun for the player yet informative for you. It can be expressed visually or with words.

Write two questions: an opening question and a follow up question, dependent on the answer chosen by the player.

The A versus B Quiz template is available at *http://GamificationU.com*, along with supplemental materials to help you design a better onboarding experience.

Example: Design an A versus B Quiz

Consider an auction site that attracts both buyers and sellers, which could use a quiz like the one shown in Figure 4-4.

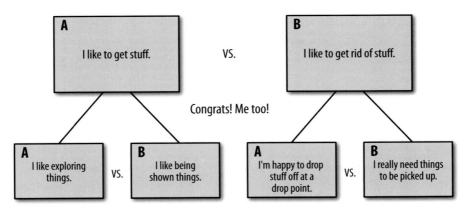

Figure 4-4. An example A versus B quiz for an auction site.

After the player answers the first question, they are given a reward statement as well as a second set of choices.

In this example, there's a tacit acknowledgement that the better we are at assessing the needs and wants of our players, the more likely we are to retain them. When your site is made up of a humongous pile of possible options behind the scenes, questions like these can help improve your players' experiences from day one and avoid frustrating with choice.

The Onboarding Challenge

To recap, if we execute our onboarding process well, we can accomplish a few key things in the first minute (or two):

- Reveal the complexity of the system slowly
- Reinforce the user positively
- Remove opportunities to fail
- Learn something about the players

Without a doubt, this is one of the most challenging and complex aspects of gamification to get right. Accomplishing all four objectives in the first few minutes may be nearly impossible in your environment, but we highly encourage you to try. The benefits of doing this right are substantial for your long-term success.

Challenges and Quests

Challenges and quests give players direction for what to do within the world of the gamified experience. After all, how much fun would a scavenger hunt be if you were told to just go and find some stuff? Nothing specific…just stuff. There isn't much of a challenge there. There is zero intrigue and an absolute lack of structure.

Some people enter the game with no idea of its goals or fundamental drives. So, even if a challenge isn't at the front and center of the experience, using challenges as an option somewhere in the body of the system can add depth and meaning for the player. *Chocolatier* is a game that has a great and satisfying set of challenges always at the ready (see Figure 4-5). Similarly, *FarmVille*'s badge/ribbon interface is a kind of challenge window, presenting an ever-scrolling list of activities that players can take to move forward.

Figure 4-5. Chocolatier offers players an almost limitless set of challenges.

The idea is to ensure there is always a challenge for players to take (ideally, you'll offer a few). Players should be able to come into the experience and always have something interesting and substantial to accomplish or try that is on your intended path for their overall experience. Some players will play challenge after challenge in sequence, trying to vanquish as much of the game as possible. Others will just try one as needed to maintain interest. Your job is to craft a large volume of interesting options.

 Note. *The player should not be given master level challenges as a novice. Different challenges for different levels are appropriate and fundamentally more successful.*

Cooperative Quests

Cooperative questing experiences, as they are known, depend on a community of players. These are the most difficult type of quest to build. In organizing a soccer game, for example, the challenge is not in finding a pair of goal posts or a ball, it's in getting 22 people to show up at the same time and play.

In the beginning of the design process for a gamified system, it is better to design a single-player game that can evolve into cooperative play as the player gains mastery and more players join the game. In this vein, Gowalla offers a series of challenges and quests a player can follow at her leisure. It isn't that she checks into a place because she is there, but that she can complete a challenge after she checks in. She can even announce her own quests and complete them for rewards. For example, she can commit to walking 12 km for breast cancer. She checks in at one end and then checks in 12 km later. Her friends know about her achievement, and the player takes pride in her accomplishment.

Obviously, cooperative designs are more socially powerful. The flip side of the soccer example we gave (which has a high minimum bar) is that the social/reward power of the experience (lots of people) also tends to increase. If your community already has a large number of active players, you should strongly consider designing something cooperative. You can also design for single-player experiences in a group context, where players act alone but their achievements roll up to a group, or the results are shared/scored with a group. Sometimes even just having the rewards doled out in a group setting can be enough to trigger that response.

Another example is fast food chain Taco John's (Figure 4-6), which uses an adaptation of *MyTown* to offer players challenges they can complete for points and free food. Challenges grow from single-social to multiplayer-social with increasing complexity.

Figure 4-6. Taco John's challenges reward players with free food and points.

As an example of single-player challenges in a group context, Jimmy Choo ran a successful promotion with Foursquare to announce its new casual footwear line for women. Players who checked in at the right time could win one of six pairs of these not-yet-released shoes. There was an axis benefit: while the prize was valuable, status was the driver. How compelling for players that only six people worldwide were going to have those shoes!

Another example, mentioned on the sidebar on page 25, is the fitness program created internally for NYC-based marketing company, NextJump, where employees who worked out the most were offered a cash prize (measured by check-ins at a company gym). This simple design got 12% of employees to exercise, and participation grew to 70% when the company made the competition team-based. The power of group reinforcement is so powerful that despite a decline in the expected reward (more people splitting the pot), engagement shot up substantially.

Create the First Challenge

Compose the first challenge after your player is onboarded. You can find examples online at GamificationU.com.

Hint: Scavenger hunts, tag, and exploration are good go-to options.

Social Engagement Loops

Social engagement loops, while not exclusive to games, borrow heavily from a viral loop design. A designer must not only see the way a player engages with the system, but also how he leaves it and—perhaps even more importantly—what brings him back again.

In a social engagement loop, a motivating emotion leads to player re-engagement, which leads to a social call to action, which flows to visible progress and/or rewards, which loops back around to a motivating emotion. Figure 4-7 illustrates this concept.

Figure 4-7. A social engagement loop, designed to maximize player engagement and reengagement using core product design.

Engagement Loop Examples

The best way to design the intrinsic virality in your gamified system is to think about the social engagement loop at various points along the progress to mastery we described earlier. Below, we've used the example of Twitter and unpacked how the viral loops work for this popular communications platform.

Novice Players of Twitter

For novice players of Twitter, the view of the engagement loop is as follows:

- Motivating emotion = Connecting and expressing
- Player reengagement = @Mentions
- Social call to action = Tweets
- Visible progress/reward = Followers

In summary, a novice player of Twitter will decide that she wants to connect and express what she thinks. Once she has done so, she may leave the system; however, if someone mentions her in a tweet (known as an @mention), she will reengage with the system. This then leads her to tweet back in response to her @mention. As a result, she gains followers because people on the site find what she has to say relevant or interesting. Thus, she is motivated yet again to connect and express herself.

Expert Players of Twitter

The game for a novice player always varies slightly from the game played at the expert level or beyond. So, using the same engagement loop, we will illustrate how an expert player leaves and is brought back to the game:

- Motivating emotion = Collecting and ranking
- Player reengagement = Tweets and retweets
- Social call to action = Follows retweets
- Visible progress/reward = Listing followers

In summary, an expert player will be motivated by how he ranks in the system. He will focus on how many followers he has and how that compares to other players in the game. Re-engagement, in addition to the @mentions, is going to also come from an interest in making other players' lists, showing up on leaderboards (in Klout, for example), and having his tweets retweeted. The social call to action has more depth for an expert player. As a novice, he didn't necessarily understand what a retweet was, but now he does. Finally, as his following and status in the game grows, there's a visible reward.

Note. *Here's a sobering thought: iPhone app metrics company Flurry says that after 30 days, a free iPhone app generally loses 95% of players. Gamified engagement, especially in mobile apps, is critical to ensuring your network success.*

The social engagement loop is important. As a designer, it is vital that you are clear about what kind of player engagement you are looking for, and then hone it to make sure your players come back.

Exercise: Create a Social Engagement Loop

Create a social engagement loop for your canonical player. Think of it as the first social loop in which that player will find herself.

Example: Create a Social Engagement Loop

This example will take an educational mathematics website and look at a relevant engagement loop:

- Motivating emotion = Exploration by parents and educators looking for tools
- Player reengagement = Challenges set up by the system and other players
- Social call to action = Score one another's problems
- Visible progress/reward = Accruing points for successfully completed challenges

A social engagement loop is important to design at every level of your system.

No matter how detailed or even simplistic you want your system to be, a social engagement loop can help you generate viral growth. Sometimes the loop for the novice will look similar to the expert's loop—for example, the motivating emotion is the same as the social call to action. This is OK because they don't have to be different.

In the Twitter example, @mentions and followers were present at both the novice and expert levels. If something is core to the design, its importance will reappear again and again. Creating these loops allows deliberateness, so you can focus on the things that get players involved, keep them engaged, and bring them back at every stage of development.

Customization

Customization can come in many forms; for example, a game designer might leave it to his players to dress up and trick out their avatars or virtual worlds. In most gamified systems (in comparison to games), the demand for 3D avatars is fairly low. However, even a simple player headshot and screen name can be considered an avatar, providing players with an opportunity for customization.

So while you probably don't need to worry much about customizing beach or forest scenes, allowing a player to select the color of her background or the font for her screen name can actually add value to her experience. It is also a great way for her to spend her virtual currency.

Customization Is Commitment

Twitter offers one of the simplest examples of customization as commitment. All players can change their photos and background images. Although there is no cost or gamified experience in doing so, when someone has not bothered to customize his view, it's obvious that he is exhibiting a low level of commitment to Twitter (and he may even be a newbie). Most designers believe that customization is a powerful tool for inciting commitment and engagement.

The Tyranny of Choice

But be warned, customization has a dark side. From Barry Schwartz's 2004 paper, "The Tyranny of Choice," we learn that people are most satisfied when choice increases from zero to one. Satisfaction then tends to increase proportionately to the number of options. However, he cautions, only to a point. When there are too many choices, satisfaction drops precipitously. In brief, enough choice is good—too much choice is bad.

His research divides people into two groups: *maximizers* and *satisficers* (satisfice is a portmanteau of satisfy + suffice). According to Schwartz, when looking to buy a new car, maximizers would have to see every car option available on the market before they could make a decision. Satisficers, on the other hand, define minimum criteria for choice; for example, they have $16,000 to spend on a two-door coupe. When they find the first car that meets those specifications, they simply buy it.

The research (backed up by personal observation) clearly shows that satisficers are generally happier people. So when it comes to gamified options, it isn't good to reveal the entire complexity of the system upfront. Give the player just enough choice to engage him without overwhelming him.

Customization with Apple

Apple has a very specific worldview on this—its customization choices are very limited. The sum of the choices Apple offers people buying its products basically comes down to laser engraving and white versus black. There is more customization when it comes to choosing an Apple computer—but unlike Dell.com where you find page after page of customizing options, the process is much more directed. Apple has leveraged the lessons of the Tyranny of Choice extremely well. How can you balance customization with choice overload?

Leveraging Customization

Customization is not a panacea. As Schwartz concluded, throwing a ton of options at people will not make them happy. And if you as the designer are not careful, players can be overwhelmed by a tyranny of choice. However, if you offer players a small number of well-placed customization options in the flow of your experience, you can get them to demonstrate commitment while educating them on your process. Especially if you choose to use a virtual currency, customization options will be a key way to redeem currency without hard-dollar cost.

Ultimately, however, games excel at offering players one choice at a time, and this minimization of complexity contributes substantially to their happiness.

Gaming the System

Do not be mistaken: people attempt to exploit any system in which there is something they deem of value. This should not be a blocking thought at the early stages of design. It is merely a statement of fact. Before the financial crisis of 2008, if the head of the Fed had been a game designer instead of an economist, there would have never been an assumption that a market could ever be self-policing. Instead, he would argue that there is no such thing. A system of self-policing is valuable, but it doesn't solve all problems. In the real world, we employ actual police because we need them.

Having said that, there is no such thing, in any arena, as foolproof security. People will push the margin on everything they can. In the world of gambling, for example, there is card counting—and a constant state of evolution between the cheater and the system designer.

Policing Your System

One basic way you can protect yourself is to create admin (administrative) or sysop (system operator) positions. The best part is that these roles can serve as a reward for success within your game and be "awarded" to players. Power, as mentioned, is one of the most motivating and enduring rewards in any system.

A second way to protect your system is to write great terms of service and apply those consistently in every sphere. In the lawsuit against Linden Labs, makers of *Second Life*, one of the issues to emerge was that the creators hadn't stayed consistent with their terms of service. That is, executives of the company made public statements that contradicted with the company's official terms. Ultimately, that can get you into trouble.

Legal Issues in Gamification

Along with a solid terms of service and various laws covering virtual currencies and rewards, the regulatory environment for gamification is shifting rapidly. Find more information about how the law can affect your engagement strategy by visiting *http://GamificationU.com*.

You should also seek to employ a system that allows you to control all transactions in a very finite way. For example, in almost all MMOGs, the system admins or the volunteer admins are able to stop and roll back transactions at any time, without a court or tribunal. If someone is trying to exploit your system, you have to be able to stop, give out the appropriate suspensions (with time to investigate), and then allow that player back. Give your admin and sysops the latitude to do that so that responsibility doesn't fall back on you. Allow them to look for unusual behavior, and then make sure they are able to take immediate and decisive action.

Finally, don't over think the policing components of a new design. What you can do is iterate, repeating actions again and again, making sure you pay attention to mistakes and successes so that as you learn, you grow. You cannot predict all types of exploits, and over-thinking system defense at the early stages will only reduce the virality and satisfaction of your experience. At first, focus on the novice player's needs, and build antiexploit features over time.

Agile and Gamification Design

Iteration is a core hallmark of agile design. In truth, agile and gamification have a lot in common—they both profess that any concept in a system requires repeated testing. All games should, in fact, be rife with testing loops. No gamified system should be built with a set-it-and-forget-it mentality. It doesn't work because players level out, get bored, game the system, or leave it altogether. By avoiding iteration, the system is certain to end up exactly where you don't want it to be.

In an agile design, prioritization is similarly important as it helps narrow the designer's focus to a limited number of specific items. Agile design looks for the minimum viable product before launch—what the designer and target consumer need now—knowing they can change it later.

In gamified design, an experience points (XP) system that assigns a point value to everything your player does is the absolute minimum for launch. The XP system must be able to report back about the players so that the designer can watch his engagement internally. Over time, this will transform any process. In part, it will highlight the system's top players. Players with the highest and most recent scores in a well-designed, well-balanced XP system are the most important early players in the game, potentially becoming early evangelists.

Further, the more gamified your market, the more gamification you will need in your system. If you are launching an airline, you probably need to employ a fairly evolved reward system from day one. If you are launching a community bank, on the other hand, you probably have some months or even years before the competitive pressure really gets to you.

Empty Bar Problem: Foursquare

If your system suffers from the "empty bar problem,"—i.e., you need a community of players to make your system interesting—you need gamification. It's the best way to get over the empty bar hump.

Dennis Crowley and Naveen Selvadurai started with a mobile location-based social network called Dodgeball before founding Foursquare. (Dodgeball was bought by Google and later shut down.) After finishing their stint at Google, Crowley and Selvadurai launched a new version of Dodgeball, with game mechanics, on the iPhone. They called the app Foursquare. Gamification unpacked something for Foursquare that had been missing previously. The problem, it seemed, was that it wasn't enough to have people say, "I'm here!" if there was no one around to reply, "Oh wow, me too!"

Think about how many people would need to take part in a system before there is any probability that more than one player would randomly be in the same place at the same time—let alone coordinate schedules for a drink or dinner! Just to turn a check-in on a mobile social network into a beer, consider how many variables must align:

1. I check in on my phone.

2. One of my friends is nearby.

3. She is monitoring my social feed in near real time.

4. She responds positively to my check in with an offer: "Let's have a beer later!"

5. I see her response while I still have time to act on it.

6. I have time after my meeting/event/etc.

7. I respond affirmatively, agreeing to a meeting.

8. We negotiate the time, place, etc.

9. We meet for a beer.

Dodgeball, as with almost all first-generation mobile social networks, relied on seren-dipity. It depended on the random chance of two people being in the same place at the same time, and a series of ill-defined steps to turn that check-in into a beer (or an intrinsic reward in the real world).

Fundamentally, what Dennis and Naveen did was turn a multiplayer game (mobile social networking) into a single-player game (mobile social networking), where the player competes mostly with himself/the system—earning badges and mayorships. In the first version of Foursquare, it didn't matter whether anyone was around to hear you check in.

Game designers leave nothing to chance. The entire experience of a player is in some way contrived, or at least optimized, to maximize the odds of success. Although it might seem serendipitous, it almost never is.

In a pick-up game of online poker, there is nothing coincidental about finding people already playing in a room when it's 2 a.m. in San Francisco. In the early days of those games, companies would hire people to fill the rooms so that when a player came along, there were always people ready to play. No matter your level in the game, designers made sure that a player of your ilk matched to you. If you were an expert, so was the paid player. Just like intrinsic motivation, you can't depend entirely on chance to drive your market. These are things gamification understands intimately.

If you have an empty bar problem, and you depend on a mass community of players to function, gamification can help you get over the hump. Another great example of that is the use of gamification by the blockbuster social shopping site Groupon.

Groupon

In the early days of the hit site Groupon, the company deployed something called the SOS mechanic. Basically, in order to get half off a spa service, 25 people needed to buy it. So, a motivated user would need to send out an "SOS" to all of her friends in order to drive traffic to the deal. It was a challenge. The user could "win" a treatment for half off if she could also motivate 24 other people to "win" one.

Now the mechanic isn't as important because there are enough people in most of Groupon's major markets to make their deals viable without it. But the SOS mechanic helped them overcome the empty bar problem in the early days, and it is still used when they enter a new market.

Sometimes these gamification tools are a means to an end, sometimes they are the sweetener to trigger desired behaviors, and when done right they create meaningful great long-term engagement from a player. Either way, they should be deployed with clear business objectives, a testing process that makes sense, and an eye on the future.

Dashboards

Dashboards tell designers what is happening in their economy, no matter how it is designed. It doesn't matter what kind of point system you have, because its job is to unearth correlations and anomalies among players. As an example, Zynga designers figured out that *FarmVille* players will spend $35 a month on the game, but after spending that amount, they will be much more likely to leave the game. So, prompting players to buy more cash after they spent $35 in a month was a bad idea. They discovered this by analyzing dashboard data.

Zynga tweaked the experience so that instead of asking for more money, the game asked the player to complete a challenge, invite a friend, etc., in order to advance. It is a small change, but if it's enough to move the needle a couple of percentage points and reduce churn, it's worth it.

Your dashboard ultimately protects your system. It can lead you to fresh and unexpected opportunities. Once you become familiar with the data points of your dashboard, you can watch your revenue and understand your pipeline. Especially if you are using a redeemable points (RP) system, you will need to know the value of those points and monitor inflation. You will use your dashboard to track referrals, churn, and returns, until eventually you can monitor player sentiment.

 Note. *Want to know more about dashboards and the other game elements in this chapter? Get more expert tips, interact with your peers, watch videos, and complete challenges at GamificationU.com.*

By then, you will be well on your way to maintaining a meaningful gamified experience for your players.

CHAPTER 5

Game Mechanics and Dynamics in Greater Depth

The basic game mechanics and structures described earlier in this book are the essential building blocks of any gamified experience. Points, badges, levels, leaderboards, challenges, and rewards can be remixed in limitless ways to create a spectrum of experiences. Gaining an understanding of those fundamentals (and best practices around onboarding) is a critical step in learning the necessary tools.

In addition to these core elements, there are a wide range of other, more detailed game mechanics and dynamics that can be used to enrich and deepen almost any experience. In this chapter, we'll look at many of those concepts, picking and choosing some of the most popular and useful across a spectrum of implementation categories.

Game Mechanics versus Dynamics

As you'll recall in "MDA Framework" in Chapter 3, game mechanics and game dynamics are different. Mechanics are the tools used to create games, while dynamics are how players interact with game experiences. We'll be looking at both mechanics and dynamics in this chapter, so pay close attention to both sides of the equation. The third part of the MDA framework, aesthetics (or how the player feels), will be described when appropriate.

Feedback and Reinforcement

One of the most straightforward and important game mechanics, and one that is increasingly a cornerstone of the gamification movement, is *feedback*. Broadly defined, feedback is returning information to players and informing them of where they are at the present time, ideally against a continuum of progress. Feedback loops are essential parts of all games, and they are seen most frequently in the interplay between scores and levels. As scores increase during an experience, they provide clear and unambiguous feedback to the player that she is heading in the "right" direction. Levels and other progress mechanics help seal the deal by breaking a long arc into smaller, more achievable units.

In the Ford Fusion, as with many hybrid vehicles, feedback about how ecologically you're driving comes in the form of a small game—in this case, a plant that grows or withers based on your performance (see Figure 5-1).

 Note. *See the other in-dash driving games at GamificationU.com.*

Figure 5-1. In the Ford Fusion, drivers see a digital plant grow or wither depending on their performance.

This aspect of feedback is critical to understanding the power and success of early gamification. In many instances, such as losing weight or even writing a book, it's difficult for a player to understand where he is at the outset or during early interactions. Moreover, the length and complexity of the overall journey is such that sometimes players can be paralyzed by the seeming lack of progress.

Especially in health, education, and other "epic journey" contexts, feedback forms the most important overarching game mechanic, intricately tied to score and progress. Consider how feedback loops affect your player interactions and how you can make them better.

Choosing the Right Fun Things

Before diving into the list of possible fun mechanics/dynamics we can work with, it may be instructive to consider how to use this list creatively. After all, we can create an almost limitless set of experiences based on the core game mechanics described in Chapters 3 and 4, so how do we choose?

Why not make choosing the right game mechanics a game unto itself? In his excellent book, *Game On* (Wiley), social game designer Jon Radoff describes a game called 42 Fun Things. In his version of the game, 42 different fun interactions are listed and cross-tabbed to player motivations (such as power, curiosity, independence, etc.). With a set of 10-sided dice, you roll and brainstorm combinations of dynamics and mechanics until you've created a list as a starting point.

This is a great basic framework for iteratively working through a list of game techniques. We recommend a more stripped-down approach with a normal pair of dice and the more limited (and common) set of mechanics listed in this chapter. Table 5-1 lists the game mechanics/fun interactions most frequently used in gamification, which can be referenced by the dice roll (roll both dice together or one alone). Combine two of the mechanics for even more fun and a greater challenge. And, as Radoff points out, you can download a dice-roll app from most mobile app stores if you don't have some dice conveniently laying about.

We highly recommend covering the mechanics in the three example columns listed in Table 5-1 while playing, so that you let your mind work creatively on the list at first. You may also find that you occasionally roll a mechanic that doesn't seem to fit your product/service or idea. Leverage that creative dissonance to your benefit and try to come up with a truly interesting way to work that idea into your experience.

Note. *There are many great lists of mechanics and dynamics across a spectrum of resources. From Jon Radoff's* Game On *(Wiley), to Jesse Schell's* The Art of Game Design: A Book of Lenses *(Morgan Kaufmann), to countless sites, titles, and companies in between. We've decided to choose a core set that is taken from a wide range of superb thinkers and the real-world experiences of social game design interaction. The mechanics listed in Table 5-1, and the dynamics themselves, are not intended to be exhaustive.*

Combining Mechanics with Social

Because socializers account for the majority of player types and motivational states, one of the most common needs is to combine game mechanics with social interactions. Moreover, socializing key game mechanics can make your experience more viral. Even if the mechanic is more achievement- or exploration-oriented, you have the option of increasing sociability to broaden its reach and cyclicality. When you play Radoff's game, consider how to make each mechanic more social.

Table 5-1. Example game mechanics.

Dice roll	Things people like	Example mechanic*	Example mechanic*	Example mechanic*
1	Pattern Recognition	Memory-game interactions: items are revealed, then hidden, then combined	Combine like items, as in object-matching games	Earn and burn: learn how to optimize virtual economies
2	Collecting	Collectible objects, such as stamps and badges	Scarcity and return: limited-availability items, time-based items	Trading mechanisms with others
3	Surprise and Unexpected Delight	Slot machines, variable reinforcement	Easter eggs, geocaching, hidden objects	Unexpected dynamism, such as Foursquare's unique and funny badges
4	Organizing and Creating Order	Time/job/throughput challenges, such as in *Diner Dash* or *Chocolatier*	Combining like items and/or creating symmetry	Organizing groups of people, like a team
5	Gifting	Easily transferrable virtual items	Gift reminders and recommendations	Karma points: only purpose is as a "gift"
6	Flirtation and Romance	Poking, smiling, flirting: lightweight, easy-to-ignore interactions	Hot or Not style: choose people from a list/group and express interest	Virtual items or lightweight "props," shout-outs
7	Recognition for Achievement	Badges, trophies	Contests, game shows, award shows	Kudos system for reinforcement, e.g., Nike Plus and Lance Armstrong
8	Leading Others	Team-based or cooperative challenges	Levels associated with leadership	Long-term, "great" challenges that require multiple players
9	Fame, Getting Attention	Leaderboards based on player feedback, scores, and promotion	Award shows, game shows, contests	Large or out-of-scale promotional opportunities, e.g., images on Flickr's home page
10	Being the Hero	"Rescue the maiden" challenges	Friends ask for help, you respond with help	MacGruber: things are going to blow up in 10…9…
11	Gaining Status	Badges, trophies—especially public ones	Scarce, limited-edition items that are public	Public, obvious scores and leaderboards
12	Nurturing, Growing	Tamagotchi style: feed this thing regularly or it will die	Points that expire in the absence of activity, growth	Pyramid scoring, with cumulative scores for teams and leaders

* Cover these columns with a sheet of paper first and reveal as needed

Game Mechanics in Depth

Most of the game mechanics in Table 5-1 can be useful and interesting to your gami-fied system. Understanding when and how to use them can be daunting, so we've provided some depth here on each of these interactions.

1. Pattern Recognition

Pattern recognition is the dynamic user interaction most associated with unpacking systemic complexity. When players seek to understand the world around them, and discover the "hidden meaning" or ways that complex items interact, they are seeking pattern recognition. Once patterns are detected, players organize the world around those patterns, and they usually feel intrinsically rewarded just for having discovered them.

As an example, consider people standing on subway platforms. If you ride a particu-lar subway system regularly, you recognize certain patterns about where to stand to optimize both getting a seat and exiting the subway at your destination (see Figure 5-2). Although we are never explicitly taught to seek this optimization, and many of us do not act on the impulse every working day, achieving this kind of knowledge or mastery is both reassuring and positive for a subway rider. Essentially, riders have lev-eled up if they know where and when they can get a seat or exit a crowded station a few minutes faster.

Figure 5-2. Pattern recognition: the advanced subway rider knows where to stand to get a seat or to be close to the right exit (image licensed under CC; photo by http://www.flickr.com/photos/piercedavid).

Exit Strategy, shown in Figure 5-3, is an application that lets players know where to be to best exit the subway. It takes ad hoc knowledge from users/maps and makes it publicly available. It can't help you get a seat, though.

Figure 5-3. Pattern recognition: the advanced subway rider game, Exit Strategy.

For pattern recognition, there are a number of game mechanics we can use to create player engagement. Some of the most common are:

Memory-game interactions

For example, the card-matching memory game we grew up with, where like objects are revealed to players and then must be remembered.

Combining like items

> Such as gem-matching games (e.g., *Bejeweled*), where successful combinations result in game advancement.

Earn and burn

> Where players discover, then master, the complexity of economic systems (usually currency-based) to optimize their score. When using virtual economies, complexity can be limitless, which can be both an opportunity and a threat.

2. Collecting

Collecting is one of the most powerful instincts among humans. Despite this strong proclivity, few rigorous studies have been done to identify the motivations behind collection.

However, one of the most interesting taxonomies of the impulse to collect comes from James Halpern, the noted futurist, author, and auctioneer. He identifies 10 main reasons people collect:

- Knowledge and learning
- Relaxation and stress reduction
- Personal pleasure (including appreciation of beauty and pride of ownership)
- Social interaction with fellow collectors and others (i.e., sharing pleasure and knowledge)
- Competitive challenge
- Recognition by fellow collectors and perhaps even noncollectors
- Altruism (since many great collections are ultimately donated to museums and learning institutions)
- Desire to control, possess, and bring order to a small (or even a massive) part of the world
- Nostalgia and/or a connection to history
- Accumulation and diversification of wealth (which can ultimately provide a measure of security and freedom)

Obviously, these motivations overlap with many of the game dynamics and motivational states we've discussed throughout this book. Perhaps the omnipresence of collecting and its breadth of reasons are why it features so prominently in gamified design. Consider mapping your collection mechanics to the Bartle personality types described in earlier chapters to best align the collection design to your audience.

Some example mechanics that can be used to "juice" collecting behavior include:

Collectible virtual objects

Items such as stamps and badges are obvious prerequisites for and foundational to a collection-based ecosystem. The fact that they can be virtual (and tied to complex economics) is one of the major disruptors present in gamified systems.

Scarcity

In order for objects to be valuable, there must be some scarcity. This scarcity is always contrived in gamified design, but it can be based on a number of factors, including player behavior and economic need.

Return

Collectible items can be tied directly to time behaviors (usually in service of your engagement metrics, such as Monthly Average Users in the Facebook context) so that you can only earn them if you take part at specific times.

Trading mechanisms

By including more complex economic systems, such as trading, you can facilitate more complex collecting behavior. Players can leverage one another to manage and increase their collections, optimizing their experience. However, trading systems expose your virtual economy to peer-controlled forces, so be sure you're ready for the effects of this choice before you make it.

As an example of scarcity, GetGlue offered limited-edition badges (see Figure 5-4) to players who checked in (in real time) for the premiere of the new *Dr. Who* series.

Figure 5-4. GetGlue issued highly collectible badges in the form of stickers for the new season of Dr. Who.

3. Surprise and Unexpected Delight

The world is full of surprises, and we can all remember instances when we were truly delighted by something unexpected. This kind of serendipitous enjoyment can and should be baked into your experience to create lasting engagement with your players. The form it takes can range from the sublime to the ridiculous, and some applications and designers have used it to great effect.

In nongame contexts, Apple is famous for designing its packaging with an element of surprise. In fact, Apple "unboxing" slideshows routinely get millions of views on the Web, causing consumers to be competitive about their unboxing "tableaux." In applications like Foursquare, the entire feedback system (badges) is designed with some degree of surprise in mind. While its badges—and indeed all badges—may feel routine, Foursquare takes pride in constantly revealing a new, interesting, and unexpected item.

Examples of mechanics that leverage surprise and unexpected delight include:

Slot machines
> Masters at variable reinforcement, slot machines make all outcomes, including wins and losses, feel unexpected—even if they're not always delightful.

Easter eggs, geocaching, hidden objects
> These mechanics place unexpected items in unexpected places. Sometimes players are explicitly informed to search for them, but more often than not, players learn about Easter eggs from a carefully constructed onboarding process and thoughtful progression.

Unexpected dynamism
> Foursquare's unique and funny badges can add some levity and break up the monotony of certain experiential systems. For example, badges that generally measure progress but then suddenly "reward" the player for having great hair are an example of surprising and—dare we say—delightful experiences.

Foursquare's Douchebag badge is controversial, but it's certainly attention-getting (see Figure 5-5). Players are not able to earn this traditionally (the location and classification of "douchey" venues is mostly proprietary), so it breaks up the monotony of the Foursquare badging system very effectively.

Figure 5-5. Unexpected dynamism: Foursquare's Douchebag badge.

4. Organizing and Creating Order

Many players are attracted to the idea of organizing things into neat, orderly sets. Not unlike collecting, this drive tends to be rewarded at the end of a particular loop or level. Some games and game-like experiences exploit this in a very unstructured but suggestive way. For example, *SimCity* allows players to express whatever level of order on their created world they believe is appropriate. Many players would choose to design highly structured and organized cities, even though there was no explicit reward or benefit to doing so in the game. Apparently it was for the players' own enjoyment, or possibly to get back at undisciplined urban planners.

Some classic examples of mechanics designed to bring out the organizer and order-creator include:

Time/job/throughput challenges
> In games like *Diner Dash* and *Chocolatier,* being able to quickly organize your routine leads to highly optimized results—i.e., group like tables together and serve more customers.

Combining like items
> Tasks that require pattern-matching as well as creating symmetry, in contexts like jewel-matching games (e.g., *Bejeweled*).

Organizing groups of people
> One example of this is cooperative or team-based challenges. This design lends itself both to the social/leadership-oriented, as well as to the organizationally oriented. A great example of this can be seen in fantasy sports or Facebook games like *Mafia Wars*, where teams with specific skills need to be organized effectively to win.

5. Gifting

Gifts form a core part of cultures across the globe, with complex and often conflicting views on process and propriety. Some countries, like South Korea and China, have a depth and propensity to gifting, so it's no wonder that the panoply of virtual gift concepts originated there.

Whereas in the U.S. and most of Europe, gifts are generally given only for major holidays and life events, in the online world, gifts are increasingly used as a regular expression of connectedness and as a core method of socialization and virality in the design itself. Consider social games, like *Café World*, that use gifts ("Susan just gave you a cake") as a mechanism for recruitment and promotion, and you understand the power of gifts in this new context. They don't need to be costly or even that thoughtful, but they should be fun and easy.

Key mechanics that support gifting include:

Easily transferrable virtual items
> Such items form the foundation of a gifting system or culture, and should be tightly integrated into the game's economy.

Gift reminders and recommendations
> These can be a systemic way to ensure that gifts are given. For example, Facebook's birthday reminders are an excellent mechanic that promotes interaction and return usage.

Karma points
> A type of point system described in Chapter 3, karma points are given to other players as a reward for something they've done. They act as a gift in a social context.

6. Flirtation and Romance

Flirtation and romance don't need to be literal expressions of sexual interest—they can serve as a friendly and engaging way to make small talk. As can be observed on sites like OMGPOP (*http://www.omgpop.com*), the option to flirt in a safe way is often more valuable than the mechanism for actually meeting (which is notably absent from such sites). The lack of need to follow through often differentiates the game mechanic of flirting from actual flirting, the opening gambit in real romance… though they may end up in the same place.

Any kind of lightweight, nonconfrontational social interaction can be considered flirty or romance-inducing. Obviously, more explicit romantic interactions can be included in gamified systems, but merely creating the potential for romance is generally sufficient. Player-matching systems that bring users together around a common idea or level of expertise are good examples of these interactions. Remember: in cultures with great social distance (including the United States), an element of flirtation can be critical for forming viral, social loops.

Game mechanics commonly associated with flirting and romance include:

Poking, smiling, flirting
> These lightweight, easy-to-ignore interactions are among the most common expressions of this idea in a dispersed social group setting. Originating in dating sites, the concept has broad appeal and can be found in most gamified systems.

Hot or Not-style
> Look at people, one by one, and (anonymously, without repercussion) decide whether you like them. If you do, they see your interest and can make contact with you.

Virtual items

Such as flowers, cards, and hearts, these items express affection or romance. Among younger audiences, particularly girls, these demonstrable items can be elemental.

Lightweight "props," shout-outs

These are platonic ways to express affection or flirtation. Karma points, stickers, and even star-rating systems can have elements of this if player opinion/feedback is not private.

Players should also be allowed to flirt with ideas and experiences—not just other players. Although this doesn't produce positive feedback loops in most cases, it can be extraordinarily useful to you.

Poking, the equivalent of a wink or flirt on most dating sites, is among the most powerful examples of the lightweight, nonconfrontational social interaction espoused in this section (see Figure 5-6).

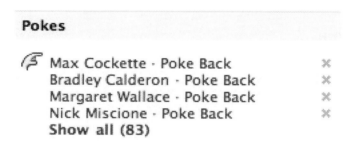

Figure 5-6. Flirtation and romance: "poking" in Facebook. You can choose to reciprocate or not, without repercussion.

7. Recognition for Achievement

Being recognized for achievement is a core desire that is reflected in almost all humans. Achievement- and killer-oriented types (per Bartle's classification) are substantially more likely to care about this kind of recognition, but it affects all players. Like collecting, achievement-recognition mechanics are among the most frequently seen in gamified design, and they can be found in a broad range of experiences.

Note. *The more public the achievement, the more valuable it is to players, particularly those who are highly achievement-oriented.*

While there is an extraordinary range of possible options for expressing achievement, some of the most popular mechanics include the following:

Badges, trophies

> These are the most common recognition items found in games because of their versatility and flexibility. If they're well designed, they can be fine-tuned in almost limitless ways.

Contests, game shows, award shows

> These can be used to socialize achievement in bigger-bang ways that tend to attract more attention than individual activities. The site Youare.tv offers a good example of newer-style game shows that leverage gamification.

Kudos systems

> These are generally used to provide positive reinforcement in the form of karma points or stars given from one player to another. There are also higher-impact forms—for example, Nike Plus and the Lance Armstrong "congratulations" announcement that players receive when achieving certain milestones (see Chapter 6).

8. Leading Others

Many kinds of giftedness are recognized in children, including mathematical, linguistic, musical, athletic, and a number of others. One of the most surprising to nonpsychologists is leadership ability. This specific skill set is poorly understood, but it has come under increased scrutiny in recent years because it is a great predictor of success.

While many players shy away from leadership-oriented challenges and opportunities, those drawn to leadership rewards are most often engaged with game mechanics such as:

Team-based or cooperative challenges

> Games that require a team to play (canonical examples include *Mafia Wars* on Facebook, fantasy sports, or actual sports). Team and co-op play can be integrated into almost any experience, but care should be taken before making team play a required element, as it increases friction for players..

Levels associated with leadership

> These are specific progress mechanics that are displayed/awarded for performance based on team and leadership vectors. Create these reward opportunities to engage leadership-driven players.

Long-term, "epic" challenges
> For example, any one player would find it difficult to sequence new genomes working alone, but collaborators should feel part of a group working toward that goal. Identifying and promoting leaders generally makes the team excel and facilitates cohesion.

9. Fame, Getting Attention

As with achievement-recognition, fame and attention-getting are important drivers for achievers and killers. Fame, however, has an added dimension: players need not achieve something on a progression scale to get it. Sometimes, a single action can produce a fame result, such as your photo showing up on the home page of Flickr. Regardless of how it's achieved, fame's metric is based on how many people view, favor, subscribe, watch, talk about, tweet, or otherwise *socially endorse* someone.

Any product or service that has ranking, points, and favorites is likely to produce a fame or attention-getting loop. YouTube is a great example of this. While fame-seeking will naturally occur, designing a virtuous loop for fame can be a double-edged sword. If you attract too many people seeking fame before you have enough platforms to promote them, you may discourage those players.

Examples of game mechanics that speak directly to the desire for fame and attention include:

Leaderboards based on player feedback, scores, and promotion
> As seen on YouTube and other highly social systems, the more others socially endorse someone or something, the more famous it can become. Remember: this can be both positive and negative.

Award shows, game shows, and contests
> These can create opportunities for fame and attention-seeking behavior.

Large or out-of-scale promotional opportunities
> Like having your photo show up on Flickr's home page, these promotions tend to combine a degree of chance (or slot-machine mechanics) with the desire for fame. Some Tumblr blogs that feature people also produce this result. The buzzy social reaction, "Did you see that Susan was featured on the home page?", is akin to getting press exposure, which can be very powerful.

10. Being the Hero

Classic game designers viewed this as one of the core motivations they designed for, especially in the male, 18–35 year old adventure-game demographic. The concept of heroism in game design is deeply ingrained, and many of the most popular arcade and console games are based on a similar rescue-the-maiden concept.

Today, and especially in gamified design, the concept of heroism is more diffuse and often more social. Instead of single-player and machine-driven affirmation of great work, hero behavior is often structured as part of a virtuous social cycle. It can be used powerfully to recruit new players and to give peer-to-peer rewards.

The popular Facebook game, *Café World,* successfully uses lightweight heroism for social promotion (see Figure 5-7). You ask friends for help and they come to your rescue—in the process, they become players.

David needs some help filling his drawers!

David's Collection Cabinet is a little sparse! Send him any of the following items for his Café: a Salad Bowl, a Salad Plate, a Serving Dish, a Soup Bowl and a Sauce Pan; David may return the favor!

3 minutes ago via Café World – the Restaurant Game · **Comment** · **Like** · **Send**

Figure 5-7. Being a hero: Café World uses much simpler acts of heroism and simulated altruism than classic "rescue the maiden" videogames.

Examples of game mechanics that leverage our desire to be heroes include:

"Rescue the maiden"
>   In the classic game sense, players are tasked with completing a set of challenges to ultimately free or be reunited with something they love. In design, it is part of an epic challenge modality.

Friends ask for help, you respond
>   As in the *Café World* example shown in Figure 5-7; this mechanic can also serve as a powerful tool to promote and recruit players.

MacGruber: things are going to blow up in 10…9…
>   The system's design challenges you to complete some simple actions in a limited amount of time. This is exceptionally powerful when combined with a team task, allowing one person to express heroism with more complete social feedback.

11. Gaining Status

Status drives much of our actions, and it forms a critical part of how we understand ourselves in context and relation to others. Status is so ingrained in our society that even those who renounce the system often derive their sense of self from the degree to which they reject it (e.g., anarchists, punk rockers, bike messengers). But while status is a big, complex, and omnipresent human desire, it can be understood simply as a system for determining where and how we fit into a hierarchy.

Elsewhere, we've discussed the extent to which status drives our behaviors across complex gamified systems like frequent-flyer programs. And while the subject has been well explored in this book thus far, it's worth noting some of the more common mechanics used to facilitate the acquisition and promotion of status in gamified systems. What all these examples have in common is that the more public they are, the more effective they are at communicating status. While status systems can work in a single-player game, they are much more effective when reinforced continuously in a competitive and public environment .

Some status game mechanics include:

Badges, trophies, levels
> Probably the most broadly used and well-understood status systems, these progress mechanics need not be seen in direct comparison to others as long as the relative hierarchy is known. For example, American Express Black Cards are understood to be rare, so their holders know they sit atop the hierarchy even without seeing what credit card is in other people's wallets.

Scarce, limited-edition items
> Items like special cars or virtual goods—especially those associated with luxury brands or self-evident scarcity—can, in the possession of their owners, be powerful symbols.

Priority access
> Red carpet lanes and unique rooms in virtual environments are great examples of obvious status mechanics that can be powerful motivators when used correctly. But in order to convey status, they must generally be activated/delivered in public. The effect you seek is more akin to a VIP area in a nightclub rather than the private dining room atop a corporate skyscraper.

12. Nurturing, Growing

While not everyone is equally predisposed to nurturing, some players are very attracted to the concept. In popular social games like *FarmVille*, "natural cycles" of nourishment and growth are a core part of the experience. Land must be tilled, seeds must be purchased, and water must be applied for growth to occur.

It's no wonder that other gamified experiences make use of the same concept. Whether it's a business that needs to grow, a virtual pet that needs regular support to thrive, or team members that need discipline and guidance, this drive is powerful in many of us.

Some example game mechanics that use growth and nurturing effectively to further engagement include:

Tamagotchi-style

Feed this thing (virtual pet, crop, etc.) regularly or it will die. This approach strongly promotes repeat visits and a sense of accomplishment.

Points that expire

Programs that require you to check in (or act) regularly to maintain your points invoke a nurture response in players, not dissimilar to the Tamagotchi play detailed above, but expressed more rationally. The most common form is airline miles that expire if you take no action in 18 months.

Pyramid scoring

Cumulative scores for teams and leaders encourage nurturers and growth-oriented socializers to invest in others. Cooperative experiences generally promote this concept with great success.

Virtual pet games, such as *QuantaPet*, encourage players to return regularly to care for their pet (see Figure 5-8). Although this interaction alone isn't enough to sustain most gamified experiences, it can form an important part of "the grind," or the regular activities a player must take to advance in the game.

Figure 5-8. Nurturing: QuantaPet requires to you to return regularly to ensure your virtual pet is generally well cared for.

Putting It Together

The detailed game dynamics and mechanics explained in this chapter can help you take your gamified design to a deeper level. By matching Bartle's user motivational state to game dynamics, we can develop experiences that target specific player behavior, resulting in greater engagement. Putting these mechanics together in sophisticated systems—which socializers, explorers, achievers, and killers can master—is the best way to advance gamification for your product, service, or brand.

In each case, the mechanics that map to the specific motivational states and drives will differ. Obviously, the aesthetic implementation will vary as well, and it should largely hew to your narrative theme and authentic brand voice—i.e., don't build a virtual pet experience if your product and market aren't suited for it. You can, however, leverage the mechanics of virtual pets to bring consumers back at regular intervals for appointments and meaningful social interactions.

 Note. *Find out more about game mechanics at GamificationU.com, where you can watch exclusive videos with key industry experts, download supplemental materials, take challenges, and interact with your peers.*

In the next chapter, we'll take a closer look at some example sites and apps that do a great job of leveraging these game mechanics, dynamics, and aesthetics in their nongame contexts.

CHAPTER 6

Gamification Case Studies

In the previous chapters, we focused on the theory and mechanics behind gamification. We looked at the psychological motivations that drive player behavior, and we analyzed the different types of players and how to design for their engagement. We reviewed key game mechanics and dynamics, and we examined how they can be used to engage players more deeply.

Game and user experience designers have been implementing these techniques for decades to create addictive games and engaging player experiences. However, gamification as a complete concept—actively relying on game mechanics to engage players and solve problems—is still in its infancy. It can be challenging to think about how they apply to disparate real-world websites and applications.

Yet, there are already a number of examples of great gamified experiences. In this chapter, we'll study several of them in depth to see what they teach us about putting gamification theory into practice.

Foursquare

Since we've mentioned Foursquare examples throughout this book, we don't include any in this chapter. But it is a perfect app to study because of its breakout gamification success, especially for its use of overt game mechanics to solve a problem—e.g., getting players to check in to a location-based mobile game. It's worth noting again that it was born from the ashes of Dodgeball, an SMS-based app that had much the same functionality but failed to keep enough players engaged. Foursquare's incredibly successful implementation of the core mechanics—points, levels, badges, and leaderboards—is worth considering when thinking about how to create a gamified user experience.

Nike Plus: Making Fitness Fun

According to the Centers for Disease Control, more than two-thirds of American adults are overweight or obese, and fewer than 20% get enough exercise. From these statistics, it's clear that physical fitness could be a lot more engaging.

Nike Plus is a social running game. The most current version is an iPhone and web application that employs sophisticated game mechanics to encourage runners—both casual and hardcore—to compete and improve their fitness program. It's a wonderful example of what great gamification can do to motivate players.

An Application for Runners

While Nike's goal was to generate brand loyalty and ultimately sell more sporting equipment, clearly it thought very carefully about what kinds of people would use the application and prioritized those players' needs first. It didn't simply start assigning points and badges for buying Nike products; instead, it sought to make running more fun and thereby attract a large community of runners to whom it could then market Nike products.

The core application is a handy tool for runners to track the time and distance of their runs. But the skillfully employed game mechanics take this basic pedometer and turn it into something far more social, engaging, and fun. Nike Plus subtly draws the player into the game and makes her want to come back again and again—thereby advancing her goal of becoming a better runner..

Different games for different runners

When a runner first starts to use Nike Plus, he is onboarded quickly and given an obvious first task: "Start a New Run" (see Figure 6-1). A player can jump right in and begin using the app as little more than a pedometer with a stopwatch. As a newbie, he can begin by playing against himself, competing against his best time or best distance, using a leaderboard of his runs to motivate him to keep improving. But as he continues to explore and use the application, new games are presented.

Social support and juicy feedback

Nike Plus adds a social layer to the basic run-tracking game, creating a much richer experience for its players. Runners are encouraged to connect to Facebook and post their run information to their feeds. When a player begins her run, the app posts a notice to her Facebook feed and asks her friends to cheer her on. Each time a friend "likes" the post, the app plays a burst of roaring crowd over her music, to let her know that a friend has just supported her efforts. This opens up a fun social loop that reinforces the player's commitment to her fitness program, whether she is training for a marathon or going for a casual jog.

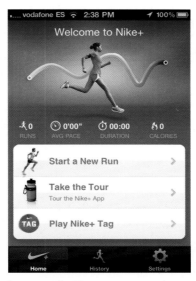

Figure 6-1. More than just a pedometer, Nike Plus uses game mechanics to keep runners motivated.

At the end of her run, the player can see the supportive comments her friends posted on Facebook. But the app also includes surprise encouragement and positive feedback from celebrities such as Lance Armstrong and Tracy Morgan, adding a variable reinforcement touch. Beautiful "heat" maps show her where she was running fastest and slowest, making it more fun and engaging to review a run.

Advanced games

An application aimed at runners can expect to draw in more competitive players, and Nike Plus does a good job of offering achievers many very satisfying ways to win. A "tag" game lets players challenge their friends to run faster or farther on their next run, or risk becoming "it." It's a clever mechanic with a built-in viral loop: once you're "it," the other players are given a "Trash Talk" wall to encourage you to start a new challenge and tag someone else.

Players with a Nike Plus web account can log into the site and join challenges (as shown in Figure 6-2) started by other runners around the world. They can also create a new challenge. Since both Nike and the running community create the challenges, there are lots of ways to win. These include posting near-Olympic qualifying times in a 5k run, or running as part of a larger group. While multiple leaderboards (including a social leaderboard) could improve the experience further, there are hundreds of open challenges and many thousands of players to compete against.

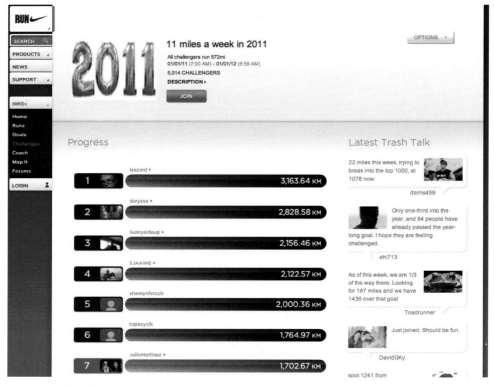

Figure 6-2. Nike Plus offers competitions so achievers can choose to compete and socialize with other like-minded players.

Continuous Evolution

Nike Plus is one of the most polished gamified experiences on the market today, in part because Nike has been continuously improving and tuning the game experience (one of the principles discussed in Chapter 4). As runners have continued to play Nike Plus, it has evolved from a fairly clunky iPod app into a sophisticated online social game.

Gamify Questions—or Answers

Subtle differences in game mechanics, such as choosing which mechanic to use and implement, can drive very different game dynamics and usage patterns. Yahoo! Answers launched in 2005 with a vision to create a community of players who would share knowledge by asking and answering one another's questions. From the beginning, it used game mechanics to drive community behavior by assigning points to actions such as answering questions, voting, and having your answer voted as a Best Answer. Levels that unlocked special powers, avatars with prominently positioned scores, and the promise of out-of-scale rewards—such as being displayed as a Featured User on the home page—created a very active community that was driven to ask and answer countless questions (sometimes over and over).

Yahoo! Answers has been a huge success. Google Answers, on the other hand, with its far less social (and much higher-friction) pay-for-answers model, closed down a year after Yahoo! Answers launched. Google Answers' small community was dwarfed by Yahoo!'s millions of daily active players.

Yahoo! Gamifies Questions

Judging by traffic and engagement, Yahoo! Answers (*http://answers.yahoo.com*) is an unqualified gamification success story. There's just one problem: it's not always the best place to find good answers (or good questions). Questions like "How is babby formed?" ricocheted around the Internet, causing teachers to cringe at many of the selected Best Answers.

 Note. *Know your meme: visit* http://GamificationU.com *for more on "How is babby formed" and to get the best additional insight to help you gamify your service.*

A closer look at its game mechanics reveals that Yahoo! Answers has always been tuned to reward community participation, rather than great answers. The experience point system did offer the biggest prize to players whose answers were selected as the best (10 points per Best Answer, with up to 50 bonus points for receiving a thumbs up from other readers). But winning the Best Answer game was time-consuming and difficult.

In the original Yahoo! Answers point system (see Table 6-1), Level One players were limited to 10 activities per day, with questions and answers counting equally against the limit. So, at two points per answer, 10 answers were worth 20 points, with the possibility of winning a 10–60 point bonus for each one selected as best (of course, there was no guarantee your answer would be selected). However, asking 10 questions, and closing them properly, was worth a guaranteed 60 points (5 points for each answer and 1 point for rating it). Thus, there was a strong incentive for players to ask lots of questions.

Table 6-1. In 2005, the Yahoo! Answers experience point system heavily rewarded question-asking.

Action	Point value
Begin participating on Yahoo! Answers	One time: 100 points
Choose a best answer for your question	5 points
Put the answers to your question to a vote	5 points
Answer a question	2 points
Log into Yahoo! Answers	Once daily: 1 point
Vote for a best answer	1 point
Rate a best answer	1 point
Have your answer selected as the best answer	10 points
Receive a "thumbs-up" rating on a best answer that you wrote (up to 50 thumbs-up are counted)	1 per "thumbs-up"

In addition, several game dynamics made question-asking even more appealing. Since most players used avatars in lieu of their real identity, they were free to ask any question without risking embarrassment in real life. While it is undoubtedly helpful for people to ask questions anonymously, it also led to a lot of personal advice- or opinion-seeking, such as, "I think everyone knows, but I haven't come out?" or "Am I pretty? Be honest please." These types of interactions tap into powerful hero and flirtation dynamics, but also result in a large collection of conversational questions that are not relevant to a larger audience.

Furthermore, there was very little friction when asking questions that had already been asked. Before submitting a question, the interface recommended related questions, but the suggestions were relegated to the bottom-right corner of the screen, as shown in Figure 6-3. There was no requirement to review similar questions, even if the phrasing was exactly the same, so many questions were asked and answered repeatedly. This resulted in a much lower-quality knowledge base.

Since 2005, Yahoo! has revised the point system to cause more friction when asking questions. Also, asking a question now costs five points, and closing it is only worth three points—a net loss of two points instead of a gain of six points. Limits on questions and answers per day are no longer shared, so the site now better incentivizes players to answer more questions than they ask.

The original game mechanics and dynamics used by Yahoo! Answers created a very vibrant community of players engaged in conversations about their questions, but not always seeking true best answers. Even though some of the new mechanics have been rebalanced, the community has not lost its social dynamics.

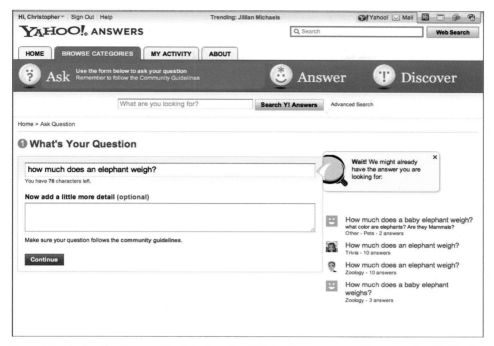

Figure 6-3. The low-friction question interface does little to discourage repeating a question that had already been answered.

The focus is still evident in the banner in Figure 6-3. The order of the calls to action still reflects the community's priorities: Ask, Answer, Discover. Asking is still the most important activity for Yahoo! Questions.

So, how could a question and answer (Q & A) site use game mechanics to relentlessly focus players on building a knowledge base of great answers? In the next section, we'll look at how Quora does just that.

Quora Gamifies Answers

Launched in late 2009, Quora (*http://www.quora.com*) is a Q&A site with the express aim of creating a social knowledge market. Players continually update and improve answers to questions with the explicit goal of having "each question page become the best possible resource for someone who wants to know about the question."

In an attempt to foster a community committed to these goals, Quora has so far been very restrictive about new sign-ups. This resulted in Quora gaining a lot of attention in 2010 for the quality of the content generated, as well as for the many high-profile people participating. However, if they achieve a very large user base in the future, they will undoubtedly face some of the quality problems that other Q&A sites have experienced.

Although the game mechanics are far less overt than they are in Yahoo! Answers, Quora has employed game mechanics that incentivize players to focus their efforts on generating really great answers. As a result, the game dynamics look very different.

Who owns a question?

There are no visible experience points to earn or lose in Quora, and a player's incentive is sharply limited by a user interface (UI) that gives very little credit and no sense of ownership to the person who asks a question. Questions are treated like communal property, which anyone can edit for clarity, ensuring that low-quality questions can be gradually improved, Wikipedia-style. Once a player asks a question, he loses control of it.

The UI strongly reinforces this by stripping status indicators from questions—i.e., a player's avatar and name are not displayed on a question page. The only way to get social credit is to generate high-quality answers (see Figure 6-4). This greatly reduces the incentive to ask bad questions.

Figure 6-4. The Quora UI offers no status for asking a question, only for answering it well.

The system also makes each question unique so that questions are less likely to be duplicated. In Quora, if a player tries to ask, "How much does an elephant weigh?", she will instead be directed to the answer. Live-updating search suggestions, which appear as players type a question, nudge them much more firmly to view a similar question before reasking it.

More controversially, Quora has tested forcing new players through a very high-friction onboarding process before they are allowed to ask a question. The first time a player tries to ask a question, he is required to successfully pass a multiple-choice test about what constitutes a well-written question, such as capitalization and phrasing, as well as what makes a reusable question. Although players have criticized this process, it is a sophisticated mechanic that trains players to play by the site's rules.

High-quality answers are the name of the game

The Quora game is won by providing high-quality answers that win the most votes for each question. The game design focuses the player very clearly on that goal. Each question page is a leaderboard, where answers are sorted in order of their vote count, not the order in which they were answered. The best answers (and the best answerers) rise to the top.

The answerer's photo, name, and bio are clearly highlighted next to her vote count, reinforcing player status in the hierarchy of answers. As a player's answer rises to the top of the rankings, so does her status. In addition, the UI provides subtle but still juicy feedback to further incentivize achievers. This includes seeing when their answers are upvoted in real-time, as well as knowing who else is currently answering the same question.

Channeling trolls and side conversations

The voting mechanism does a good job of sorting the best answers, but Quora also does a few other things that help refine the experience. Using a hero mechanic, Quora empowers players to help improve one another's posts by suggesting edits to the author of any answer. Power players, currently hand-selected, can actually edit answers; new players must have their first answers reviewed.

Not only does this help improve the answers, it goes a long way toward cutting down on spam and trolling. Quora has two other well-implemented mechanics to help control trolling and keep "killers" in line. Answers that are flagged by a reviewer, or downvoted far enough, collapse and drop to the bottom of the page. This reduces the effect of troll posts on the quality of the page by removing a great deal of the fun and attention that drives trolling behavior. While the conversation can continue (which is critical for mollifying the original poster), it does not interfere with the community.

A separate comment thread, hidden one level below the answer thread, does something similar with flirtation mechanics. Players can carry on side conversations, compliment one another, or enter into debates, but it occurs outside the main answer channel. In this way, the UI allows side discussions, giving players a social outlet to express themselves, without detracting from the page's main purpose as a knowledge resource.

So far, the result has been that even controversial topics seem to cause thoughtful answers to rise to the top, as shown in Figure 6-5, while the more belligerent troll answers and side conversations are moved one click away from the question page. By hiding these types of comments instead of relying on moderators to delete them, Quora actually channels trolls and players looking for a conversation into their own rooms, keeping the real answers front and center.

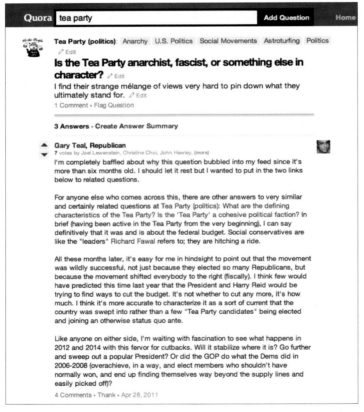

Figure 6-5. Even for controversial questions, the game dynamics drive players to give thoughtful answers and push side conversations out of sight on Quora.

As a relatively new website, Quora has not yet had to face the challenge of tens of millions of players trying to game the system, so it's too soon to declare the model a complete success. But the game mechanics employed have so far yielded an impressively high-quality set of questions and answers, as well as a community devoted to preserving it.

Health Month

Health Month (*http://healthmonth.com*) takes New Year's resolutions and turns them into a social game, helping people take steps big and small to improve their lives. Although at the time of this writing it is still a young site in beta, its rule system has been evolving through many years of play-testing (originally as a game among friends and later as a Facebook group).

A new player starts by choosing a set of self-improvement rules for the upcoming month, such as doing household chores or eating more fresh fruit. He answers detailed questions about his goal and rates how difficult he thinks it will be to achieve. Health Month uses the information to calculate the degree of difficulty and number of points to assign to each task.

Once a player is satisfied with his goals, he commits to them for the rest of the month, signing a "contract" to complete them. Game play consists of actually doing the self-improvement tasks and reporting on progress each day.

Since the purpose is to inspire action outside the game, Health Month uses a structure that is more overtly achiever-oriented than most social games. To make sure that the over-achievers do not crush the less-skilled players in the leaderboards, players are automatically grouped into brackets based on the difficultly of their monthly program.

Onboarding

Considering the complexity of the underlying game mechanics, Health Month does an excellent job of onboarding a new player by slowly revealing the entire game. The idea of starting a game that promises to help you "Live Healthier" is a high-friction moment for many people, even if it promises to be fun. The Health Month home page (see Figure 6-6) includes two possible calls to action: "Try it for free" for those ready to take the plunge, and "Spin the wheel" for those who might need more convincing about the "for fun" part.

Figure 6-6. The Health Month home page tries to convince nervous new players that getting healthier will be fun.

Spinning the wheel reveals randomized encouraging advice and product screenshots to help nudge the player into the game. While we would love to see a more enticing and fun-looking wheel, and we think the mechanic could probably be improved if it delivered a win that could be collected only by starting, "Spin the wheel" is a good tactic to convince hesitant players to try the game.

Points Systems

Health Month makes use of several point systems to nudge players toward their goals:

Points

A basic XP system rewards players for taking positive actions. As a player advances toward one of her goals, she earns points for each one she achieves, along with a bonus for doing so in a timely manner. Points for each rule are calculated based on the player's own ratings of difficulty and importance, but an achiever quickly surmises that the way to win the game is to convert to a paid plan that allows more than three rules a month. A timely login bonus rewards players who log in every day, versus batching their updates, which helps keep them active in the game.

Life points

Players also receive 10 life points at the start of each month and lose them each time they don't adhere to a rule. This type of point system is more stick than carrot, and it is seen more often in hardcore video games than in social games and gamified apps, because it can be perceived as discouraging. It works well in Health Month where, by definition, the player is aligned with the game objective to "live healthier." These points are very difficult to manage: if playing three rules, a player has 90 chances to lose a life point but only 10 life points to lose. Taking more than three days off from the game is all it takes to lose. The potential negative impact on motivation is softened since the player can continue with negative life points. He also has the chance to win extra life points randomly or via the parallel "pieces of Fruit" system.

Fruit

Pieces of fruit are earned as random bonuses and are used as karma points, existing only to be given to other players in need. Each piece of fruit that you give to another player converts into a life point for her. Since life points are so valuable, this hero mechanic encourages a strong social engagement loop, further reinforcing a player's sense of community and commitment to the game.

Spirit Dollars

Health Month also has a virtual currency, called Spirit Dollars. As of the writing of this book, Spirit Dollars are earned as a monthly bonus and cannot be spent, but the FAQ promises that a "Spirit Store" will eventually open, providing a sink for those Spirit Dollars.

Sponsorships

Sponsorships are a form of virtual gift that allow a paying player to sponsor a free player's upgrade to a paid game for one month. Paying players receive sponsorships to give away, but they can also be purchased directly or occasionally won at random. To receive a sponsorship, players have to post a public application explaining why they should be sponsored. While a sponsor can choose anyone he wants, most sponsors seem to expect applicants to prove their dedication by first playing and winning a free game. This kind of friction creates strong social bonds and a deepened sense of community.

The interlocking series of points systems yield a complex dynamic, where players are subtly nudged and prodded to engage more deeply with the site. By revealing each new system slowly, Health Month helps new players get the most out of the game without overwhelming them. A new player is trained to focus mostly on experience points, earning them for logging activities and completing goals. When a player first misses a goal, a life point is taken away, but the game softens the blow with encouragement—"Oops! Fell off the wagon. Get back on!"—and then explains the new point system: "This was an indulgence. You lost a life point. Might want to consider making a plea for some fruit from the Game Wall page." As she continues to play, she discovers her Spirit Animal, who begins by giving advice and helping to track new metrics, such as stress levels and happiness. Only at the end of the first month of play does the Spirit Animal reveal the Spirit Dollar currency.

Health Month Badges: Gaming the System

In February 2011, Health Month introduced a series of Foursquare badges, giving players the chance to earn achievements and share them with their friends on Foursquare. While the system was a success, drawing in lots of new players and providing a powerful social incentive to achieve goals, it also illustrated one of the lessons we outlined in Chapter 4: if there is something of value in a system, the system will be gamed.

Players loved the new badges and the bragging rights they afforded, but there was an unintended consequence. Because experience points are the key to unlocking badges, and paying players have far more opportunities to earn experience points, the easiest way to earn badges was to upgrade and play with a lot more rules. While this was very beneficial for Health Month—more paying players—it also had an unwanted side effect: sponsorships became a coveted tool for unlocking badges without paying. Despite heavy policing by the most engaged players, new players began to spam the forums, shamelessly begging for sponsorships instead of patiently using the application system.

As of this writing, Health Month has been asking the most passionate players for ideas in an attempt to fine-tune the system. Early attempts to solve the problem highlight how difficult it can be to deal with killers who want to win at all costs. Automatically banning the word "sponsor" from forum posts, for example, only caused a flowering of creative new spellings. Limiting the top badges to paid players, an idea now being considered, will probably ease the problem. But ultimately, Health Month will likely need to take some of the proactive steps that we discussed in Chapter 4, such as banning players and coming up with outlets for killers to express themselves without ruining the game for others.

In this way, the game weaves a complex set of scores into the game play, each one reinforcing the player's attempt to complete his monthly goals, while providing many ways to win (achieving daily goals, helping others, reducing stress, losing weight, etc.). The most advanced players join teams, where there are opportunities to socialize, lead, and help team members achieve group goals. It's a nuanced system, which has been gradually tuned for compelling game play. For motivated players, it successfully taps into psychological reinforcements that can actually improve their lives.

In fact, one of the authors of this book has been eating fresh fruit nearly every day since he started writing this case study, just to avoid losing life points. (He will also confess to some soul searching about whether guacamole really counts as "fresh fruit.")

Health Month proves that a well-implemented game design can help motivate people to make changes in their real lives.

Conclusion

In the preceding chapters, we discussed gamification, player motivations, game mechanics, and techniques. In this chapter, we looked closely at how companies have successfully used game mechanics and game-thinking to solve problems and create more engaged players. We saw how mechanics can help drive very strong community engagement, as well as how slight changes in mechanics can yield very different behaviors.

If you've made it this far, you know enough about gamification to start applying it to your own products, services, and ideas.

In the final chapters, we'll pivot toward the technology and give you some of the nuts and bolts you need to get started. We'll show you how to code game mechanics, and we'll also take a look at an off-the-shelf solution that can help you implement complex point systems.

You have everything you need to get started. Your players are waiting for you to guide them up the mountain. It's time to be their Sherpa.

Check out more case studies and get insights from gamification experts at GamificationU.com.

CHAPTER 7

Tutorial: Coding Basic Game Mechanics

Predating even the foundations of the Internet, forum software has been a basic component of networked interactions for decades. Though they've had ups and downs, forums continue to be an essential part of the interactive experience online, and they are probably already on your roadmap (if not already implemented). Most forums make use of player status to distinguish between junior and senior members, but a more explicit gamification strategy can help make standard forums more fun.

As we've seen in previous chapters, creating a truly great gamified experience involves thinking very closely about your players and fine-tuning game mechanics to engage them more deeply. In this chapter, we'll show you how to gamify a basic forums site. We'll help you get started by walking you through code examples to implement a gamification skeleton with points, levels, badges, and leaderboards. With the basic structures in place, you'll be able to iterate and fine-tune a more complete gamified experience.

Not a Programmer?

The next two chapters are clearly more technically oriented than the rest of the book, but don't despair if you're a non-programmer! You can use this chapter to think through the logic of implementing a gamified experience, skipping over the code if it's not your core strength.

As a starting point, we'll use an easy-to-set-up open source Ruby on Rails project, called Altered Beast (*http://github.com/courtenay/altered_beast*). Altered Beast is a well-coded, no-frills forums application that includes extendable basic user function-alities such as account creation and forums participation. In short, it's a perfect place to begin a gamification tutorial (see Figure 7-1).

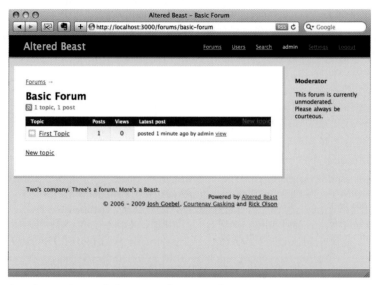

Figure 7-1. Altered Beast forums before a gamification makeover.

Planning a Gamification Makeover

Before jumping into the code, let's spend some time thinking through how we can apply game mechanics to our forums software.

All forums, regardless of theme, work best if they become online communities. Players tend to establish personas on the site and friendships are often made. Regulars check in often—sometimes dozens of times per day—to read new information, follow up on posts, and initiate conversations. New players stumble upon the forums and must be pulled in quickly by interesting content; otherwise, they may drift away.

The quality of the forums relies a lot on the quality of the players and their sense of belonging to something important. Popular forum sites take on a life of their own, with unique jargon, side conversations, and enforcement of social norms. While most forum sites offer the same basic features—creating an identity, posting topic threads, commenting on previous topics, and discovering new content—the specific implementation of these features has a big effect on how the community is formed. Turning a simple forum site into a vibrant, online community is a big project.

It requires the designer's effort and dedication, but also a substantial investment of time and energy from users. Beyond the hurdles of creating an account and verifying identity, forums only work if users follow and participate in conversations. Using game mechanics, we can turn users into players by helping infuse their identity with meaning (rank, status) and providing incentives for taking actions that will endear them to the community. Because this principal challenge is psycho-social, the power of game mechanics are well aligned with player motivations and interests, and we must focus our design on shaping their behaviors in appropriate ways. If we've done our job well, these incentives will ultimately satisfy the player, his community, and our company.

Our goals in this process should be to make using the site more fun, to incentivize players to act in the community's interest, to avoid rewarding negative behaviors, and to provide a deeper sense of status and achievement to players who participate more fully in the site.

Points and Rules

Let's start by defining some rules for earning points (see Table 7-1). Points are a simple tool to reward behavior, and they provide an excellent base upon which to build a gamified design. The first step is to define the basic activities that we want players to take. These should be easy activities that encourage players to engage with the site.

Table 7-1. Point awards for player activities.

Points	Activity	Purpose
10	Create an account	An early bonus to keep the player from starting with zero points
10	Post a reply	Encourage the player to participate
30	Start a new topic	Bonus for starting a new thread should be higher than simply replying
10	Log in once per day	Reward players for coming back to the site frequently

Agile Reactions to Gaming the System

This simple point scheme is designed around the behaviors that we (as the site's owners) believe will engender the right outcome. However, this design also creates an incentive for players to game the system (for example, by posting chaff comments to quickly earn points). For now, let's ignore the risks of malfeasance and address those (known and unknown) issues after we get our basic site live. In this way, we can preserve an agile approach to game mechanic development and focus on the first order of business: getting community built around our site.

Some countermeasures are described throughout this chapter, such as in the section "Preserving the integrity of your point model" on page 122. We encourage you to consult them as guidelines for reining in unwanted behaviors.

Table 7-1 defines a list of primary player activities on a forum site. Except for the create account bonus, these are all core activities that we want to encourage players to repeat regularly, such as logging in to check threads and participating in conversations. Together, they form the basic game play of our forum. We've included a one-time sign up bonus so that a player's first experience with the scoring system is positive and engaging. It will also encourage a curious or competitive player to begin exploring the point system—he is likely to begin hunting for information about where these 10 points came from and how to earn more.

Levels

To increase a player's competitive instinct, we can implement a series of levels that confer rank as players become more active. A good and straightforward way to award levels in a new gamified design is to base them on point thresholds. As players earn points, they move up an incremental series of levels. To infuse the level with meaning—i.e., a ranking within the system—the levels should be named in a way that indicates status. Also, the level should be displayed throughout the boards, along with the player's headshot or avatar. More complex designs, such as awarding levels based on consecutive actions or achievements, are also possible. But starting with a points-based system makes it easier to tune your new game economy after you open your doors. If you find that only 1% of your players make it to level two, you can lower the threshold without a major recode.

For our forums makeover, we'll define a few levels based on earning specific point thresholds. We need to be careful to define the levels sequentially, with appropriate minimum scores, so that the levels are indeed consecutive. Let's define a series of level scores that gradually get harder to achieve: 0, 50, 100, 200, 350, 600, 1,000, and 2,000 (see Table 7-2). We would like the player to quickly earn some status but then work harder and harder to get to the top. This will give all players a chance to feel as though they're accomplishing something, yet ensure that the most dedicated are not bored by rising up and out too quickly.

Designing Levels

Entire volumes have been written about level design. Finding the right balance between challenge and achievability is what makes level design a proprietary discipline with many skilled practitioners. As such, balancing levels in detail is outside the scope of this book, but we encourage you to iteratively test and review the effect of your levels and progress mechanics with actual players. Be flexible and make changes as needed in an agile fashion.

Table 7-2. Levels are a way to both reflect player status and encourage competitive behaviors.

Level	Name	Points required
1	Fresh Meat	0
2	New Around Here	50
3	Wallflower	100
4	Learning the Ropes	200
5	Something to Say	350
6	Know-it-all	600
7	Expert	1,000
8	Guru	2,000

Choosing Level Names

In general, you will want to give these levels names that are meaningful and fun, conveying both rank and the meaning of that rank. Many forum level-naming schemes include ranks like Newbie, Expert, Genius, and Founding Member. Take a look at your favorite forums for clues about what works in your industry and what doesn't.

Badges

Another way of explicitly nudging a player to action is to award badges for completing tasks. Badges both reward player actions and provide an additional measure of status on the site, because they give players a way to show off their accomplishments. A well-designed badge system should let the player earn a few badges easily, and then make earning them progressively more challenging. For our forums makeover, we'll set up a few basic badges, which are listed in Table 7-3.

Table 7-3. Badges for player activities.

Badges	Activity	Purpose
Newbie	Create an account	An easy badge, just to get the player warmed up
Chatterbox	Post 5 comments	Award a new player who begins to participate in a significant way
Icebreaker	Post 3 new topics	Encourage players who start new conversations
Talk of the Town	Post a topic that gets 10 comments	Reward a player for starting a particularly interesting conversation

Think of badges as a way of rewarding the player for an extraordinary achievement, such as learning a new skill. Depending on your site and your audience, a well-designed badge system can launch players into a "mission mode," where they go far and above the required effort just to earn a badge (and its concomitant bragging or laughing rights). Examples would be the Crunked badge that Foursquare awards after a player checks in at enough bars, or Gowalla's Hacker pin for checking in at 25 technology startups. Badges can even be tied to special features or privileges that are unlocked for certain behaviors—for example, a Moderator pin would give well-rated players the ability to delete comments in a forum. Badges, then, are particularly meaningful because players are doubly incentivized: not only do they receive additional powers, their pins indicate to other players that they have special privileges. A well-designed badge system can be a powerful motivator.

A System for Tracking Scores and Levels

Now that we have a basic game design in hand—with points, levels, and badges clearly defined—we can begin to modify Altered Beast. We'll start by implementing a general framework to award and track points and levels. Once that's in place, we can add business logic based on our game design.

Creating a Level Model

Let's begin by adding a few basic models and methods to award player points. To do this, we'll need to define a Levels model to track the available levels. We'll also need to modify the Player model to track points and levels.

The Levels model defines hierarchical ranks, which players achieve by earning points. While there are many ways to assign levels, in our design, we chose to award levels by cumulative points earned, which makes it easier to adjust those levels without recoding our system. Once we have more data on how our players are progressing through the levels, we can, if necessary, change the minimum or maximum points required to advance.

In Example 7-1, we define an ActiveRecord model migration to create a levels table and populate it with the levels we defined in Table 7-2.

Example 7-1. Creating a migration to define levels.

```
class CreateLevels < ActiveRecord::Migration
def self.up
create_table :levels do |t|
t.integer :number
t.string :display_name
t.integer :required_score, :default => 0
t.timestamps
end
Level.create(:number => 1, :display_name => "Fresh Meat",
 :required_score => 0)
Level.create(:number => 2, :display_name => "New Around Here",
 :required_score => 50)
Level.create(:number => 3, :display_name => "Wallflower",
 :required_score => 100)
Level.create(:number => 4, :display_name => "Learning the Ropes",
 :required_score => 200)
Level.create(:number => 5, :display_name => "Something to Say",
 :required_score => 350)
Level.create(:number => 6, :display_name => "Know-it-all",
 :required_score => 600)
Level.create(:number => 7, :display_name => "Expert",
 :required_score => 1000)
Level.create(:number => 8, :display_name => "Guru",
 :required_score => 2000)
end
def self.down
drop_table :levels
end
end
```

Example 7-1 creates a table that we can use to set levels, which will give players a way to earn rank within the community. As players earn points, we want them to level up at defined intervals, increasing their rank. Each level has a number, a display name, and a minimum score required to advance. To make this lookup easy and consistent, we'll create a convenience method to find the correct level for a given score. We'll then add this method to the Levels model:

```
def self.find_level_for_score(score)
Level.find(:first, :conditions => [ "required_score <= ?", score], :order =>
"required_score DESC")
end
```

The lookup method takes a score and returns the highest level for which it qualifies. The method will work because we defined our levels sequentially with appropriate minimum scores. As long as there is a level with a required score of zero, this method will never return a nil value.

Adding Scores and Levels to the User Model

Now that we have a model to define levels, we're ready to modify the existing player model to track the player's current score and level. We'll begin with an `ActiveRecord` migration to add these fields to the user table:

```
class AddScoreAndLevelToUsers < ActiveRecord::Migration
  def self.up
    add_column :users, :score, :integer, :default => 0
    add_column :users, :level_id, :integer
  end
  def self.down
    remove_column :users, :score
    remove_column :users, :level_id
  end
end
```

This gives us a place to track the player's score and to assign a current level. We set the default score to zero so that we don't have to worry about dealing with nil scores in our arithmetic.

Next, we'll define our model relationships. Since we've already defined a levels table with an id column, and since we added the foreign key `level_id` to the user table, Ruby on Rails makes it easy to define our table relationships. To do this, we'll add one line of code to both the User class and the Level class:

```
class User
  belongs_to :level
  ...
class Level < ActiveRecord::Base
  has_many :users
  ...
```

This describes the "User has many Levels" relationship so that we can access attributes in a very readable way—for example, by writing things like `user.level.display_name`.

Now, we have a `score` and a `level_id` attribute defined on the User model. This would be a sufficient framework to allow us to jump right into coding business logic, but there is one problem. Although we have an attribute to track a player's score, we have no way to log the activities that generated that score. This makes it hard to audit how players achieved a given score, limiting our ability to explain to players how they earned their points. Let's add one more model to log events that generate points, so that we have a history of how a player achieved her current score. It will come in handy, particularly if we need to deduct points from her score later.

Creating an Events Model

An Event model will give us a way to keep a log of each time the player earns or loses points so that we can track his point history. We'll start by adding a migration to create a table to store the event data:

```
class CreateEvents < ActiveRecord::Migration
  def self.up
  create_table :events do |t|
  t.integer :user_id
  t.string :text
  t.integer :points
  t.timestamps
  end
  end
  def self.down
  drop_table :events
  end
end
```

The Event model will store a point value and a text description of why the transaction occurred. In the model class, we need to define the "belongs to user" relationship. And for convenience, we'll also define a default sort order for events so that recent events will show up first in any listing:

```
class Event < ActiveRecord::Base
  belongs_to :user
  default_scope :order => 'created_at DESC'
end
```

That takes care of the Event model. To take advantage of Ruby on Rails' ActiveRecord code for simple lookups, we need to define the "each user has many events" relationship in the User model:

```
class User
  has_many :events, :dependent => :destroy
  ...
```

The only things we're missing now are methods awarding points to the player and updating her score.

Extending the User Model to Scores and Levels

Whenever we add points to the player's score, we'll need to check whether the player has achieved a new level. To do this, we'll include a convenience method that adds points and some private lookup methods to set the player's score and level. See Example 7-2.

Example 7-2. Extending the user model to add points and set levels.

```
class User
belongs_to :level
has_many :events, :dependent => :destroy
```

❶
```
def add_points(new_points, event_string)
update_score_and_level(new_points)
log_event(new_points, event_string)
end
private
```
❷
```
def update_score_and_level(new_points)
new_score = self.score += new_points
self.update_attribute(:score, new_score)

new_level = Level.find_level_for_score(new_score)
if new_level &&
(!self.level || new_level.number > self.level.number)
self.update_attribute(:level_id, new_level.id)
end
end
```
❸
```
def log_event(points, text)
events.create(:points => points, :text => text)
end
end
```

❶ *The* add_points *method*

The public method add_points is a convenience method that handles awarding points, updating the player's level, and logging the event.

❷ *Updating a player's score and level*

The update_score_and_level method ensures that we update a player's score and level safely. First, it increments and updates the score. We use the update_ attribute method to quickly save the score to the database without triggering any model callbacks. Next, the method looks up the level for the new score. If the player does not yet have a level—i.e., he's a new user—the new level is saved. If the player already has a level, the level is updated only if the new level is of a higher rank.

❸ *The* log_event *method*

The log_event method handles creating an event to log each change to a player's score.

With this basic framework in place, we have all the code we need to implement some game logic. Since user.add_points handles player score updates, checking for a new level, and logging the event, it will be very easy to focus on the game logic that awards those points.

Awarding Points for Key Activities

With a basic points system in place, we can now focus on awarding points for game-play behavior. In Table 7-1, we defined four conditions for earning points: signing up, replying to posts, creating posts, and logging in once per day. Because it's very likely that you'll want to change the award values for activities as part of your game-tuning process, it's helpful to define award bonuses as constants in an initializer file:

```
SIGNUP_BONUS = 10
POST_BONUS = 10
TOPIC_BONUS = 30
LOGIN_BONUS = 10
```

Using consistent constant names will make the bonus award code easier to read and modify.

Awarding a sign-up bonus

To award a sign-up bonus, we'll first need a private method in the User model. We can use a Ruby on Rails before_create callback to run a method just after a new user is created. At the top of our User model, we can define the callback and a new method to run:

```
after_create :award_signup_bonus
```

This tells Rails to execute an award_signup_bonus method just after a new user is created successfully. We can reuse the add_points method we created earlier to award the bonus in a new private method:

```
def award_signup_bonus
  add_points(SIGNUP_BONUS, "Sign-up bonus!")
end
```

The new method will be called in a transaction, right after the user record has been saved successfully. It uses our add_points method to give the user 10 points, log the event, and update her starting level.

Awarding bonus points for replying to posts

Awarding bonus points for replying to topics only takes a few lines of code as well. Altered Beast already tracks some statistics every time a new post is created, so we only need to add a callback on the Post model to award points:

```
after_create :award_user_points
```

and then define a protected method to award points:

```
def award_user_points
  user.add_points(POST_BONUS, "You posted a reply.")
end
```

That was easy! Now each time a player creates a post, we'll award him 10 points.

Preserving the integrity of your point model

There is a small catch you might notice while adding the callback. In the Post model, just below the after_create callback is an after_destroy callback. This means it's possible for a moderator or the player to delete a comment in a thread.

If we do nothing else at this point, players can earn points for comments that the moderator deems inappropriate—or they can even earn points by posting and deleting one comment repeatedly.

Countermeasures

Game mechanics are often designed to engage a player's competitive instincts. As such, your design needs to anticipate that some players will try to game the system. If you make it possible for them to cheat or earn points by repeatedly taking unhelpful actions without consequences, some players will do it. Consider building in some limits to the number of posts per day, or allowing players to flag posts, immediately removing the offending player's earned points. While the first version of your system need not consider all these issues we've noted, it's good practice to anticipate that anything that can happen will happen.

In a forum, the community will put the brakes on inappropriate behavior because truly engaged players will avoid being banned or shunned by the moderator. While more sophisticated code to limit repeated or unhelpful posts—such as rating and flagging comments—may be required in some forums, for our basic design, we just want to ensure that a player is not rewarded for malfeasance.

In this case, all we need to do is add a callback to deduct points when a post is deleted, either by the player or a moderator. To make the code more explicit, we'll first create a deduct_points method on the User model:

```
def deduct_points(points_to_deduct, event_string)
  add_points(-points_to_deduct, event_string)
end
```

This method takes a positive point value, makes it negative, and then calls the add_points method. This will allow us to write a more readable callback on the Post model:

```
after_destroy :update_cached_fields, :deduct_user_points
```

after_destroy will call a new private method on the Post model to deduct these points:

```
def deduct_user_points
  user.deduct_points(POST_BONUS, "Your post was deleted.")
end
```

The `after_destroy` callback method calls an explicit `deduct` method on the `User` model. Now, when a moderator or player deletes a post, the player's score will be reduced, which should deter overposting, but still encourage a player to post relevant comments.

Awarding bonus points for starting new topics

When a player creates a new topic, we can award and deduct points in the same way we did above for new posts—by adding new `after_create` and `after_destroy` callbacks to the `Post` model:

```
after_create :create_initial_post, :award_user_points
after_destroy :update_cached_forum_and_user_counts, :deduct_user_points
...
def award_user_points
 user.add_points(TOPIC_BONUS, "You posted a topic.")
end
def deduct_user_points
 user.deduct_points(TOPIC_BONUS, "Your topic was deleted.")
end
```

Now, when a new post is created, we add points to the player's score. If the player or moderator later decides to delete the topic, the player's points will be retracted.

Awarding a login bonus

Awarding a login bonus is a powerful way to motivate players to come back to your site frequently. Before implementing the feature, you will need to think about your site design and how players log in. In our example, players will receive a bonus when they visit the site, up to once per day. If you want players to visit your site more often, you might want to change the interval to every n hours. However, it's a good idea to limit this kind of bonus to avoid allowing players to log in and out repeatedly just to earn points.

Deciding whether the player should earn the bonus is very straightforward; the trick is deciding how often to check. A timed interval award-check line of code would look something like:

```
award_login_bonus if last_login_bonus_awarded_at > 1.day.ago
```

If the last bonus was awarded more than one day ago, the player should get a new bonus. The right place to call this line of code will depend on how your site handles sessions. If it uses sessions that expire relatively quickly, such as a bank that requires the player to log in every hour, you can trigger the bonus check each time the player logs in. As long as your sessions are shorter than your bonus limit, this could work well.

But what if your site lets players choose a "remember me on this computer" option, so that they only log in periodically? If you allow players to stay logged in to your site for longer periods of time, you will need to check `award_user_points` when a player views a page. Depending on how your site is architected, you can either insert this check as part of the session authentication, or by adding a filter to your Application Controller. The `award_user_points` method would be called every time the player requests any page.

This could be a good option if you are already caching the `user` object for authentication, or if you have no way to predict which views a player would visit. But you will need to be careful about performance because the method will be called for every single page you serve.

In the case of a forums site, the behavior we fundamentally want to reward is reading the forums, so we can cheat a little and trigger the event only when a player views a topic.

In fact, Altered Beast already uses this trick to track when a player was last seen online. Instead of updating the `user.last_seen_at` every time a player loads a page, Altered Beast does it only when she loads a new topic (via the `Topics#show` method). Because this is the same behavior we want to use as a player reward, we can piggyback off the `user.seen!` method to grant our login bonus. If your site is structured similarly, you might want to use a design such as this.

First, we need a place to store the time when the player last received a login bonus, so we'll start with a migration to add a new field to the database:

```
class AddLastLoginBonusTimestampToUser < ActiveRecord::Migration
  def self.up
    add_column :users, :last_login_bonus_awarded_at, :datetime
  end
  def self.down
    remove_column :users, :last_login_bonus_awarded_at
  end
end
```

This adds a `last_login_bonus_awarded_at` attribute to the `User` model, so we can store a timestamp when the player last earned the bonus. Next, we'll add a method to the `User` model to award the login bonus. We'll include the decision logic inside the method and also handle some errors:

```
def award_login_bonus!
  unless last_login_bonus_awarded_at \
    && last_login_bonus_awarded_at > 1.day.ago.utc

    add_points(POST_BONUS, "Daily login bonus!")
    write_attribute :last_login_bonus_awarded_at, Time.now.utc
  end
end
```

Because new players will not have a `last_login_bonus_awarded_at`, we must first check for a nil. If `last_login_bonus_awarded_at` is populated, we check whether the date is greater than one day ago. We only care about relative time—i.e., how many hours have passed since the last award. So, to avoid worrying about time zones, we'll store the "awarded at" date in Universal Standard Time (UTC).

If `last_login_bonus_awarded_at` is nil or older than one day ago, we call our `user.add_points` method and update the database. We use the `write_attribute` method once again because it performs a fast database update without triggering all of our `User` model validations.

All that's left is to insert a call to this method in the method:

```
def seen!
  now = Time.now.utc
  self.class.update_all ['last_seen_at = ?', now], ['id = ?', id]
  write_attribute :last_seen_at, now award_login_bonus!
  award_login_bonus!
end
```

Altered Beast uses the `seen!` method to update the player's `last_seen_at` date each time he views a topic. We'll check for our award bonus at the method and ensure it gets called frequently, but not on every call.

So far, we've completed a basic set of rules for awarding player points, and we've created a series of models to track the data. Next, we'll display some of this data to provide feedback on how players are doing.

Badges

Now that we've implemented code to award points and increase levels as players earn more points, we might logically want to award badges for extra achievements. Back in Table 7-3, we defined four types of badges. To award those badges, we'll first need a `Badge` model to define the types of awards. Example 7-3 shows the code for creating this model.

Example 7-3. Creating a Badge model.

```
class CreateBadges < ActiveRecord::Migration
  def self.up
  create_table :badges do |t|
  t.string :name
  t.string :display_name
  t.timestamps
  end

  Badge.create(:name => "newbie", :display_name => "Newbie")
  Badge.create(:name => "chatterbox", :display_name => "Chatterbox")
  Badge.create(:name => "icebreaker", :display_name => "Icebreaker")
  Badge.create(:name => "talk_of_the_town", :display_name => "Talk of the Town")
  end
  def self.down
  drop_table :badges
  end
end
```

The Badge model functions much like our Level model, defining a range of possible awards that a player can receive. Unlike levels, players can have many badges at one time. This sets up a many-to-many relationship between badges and players, so we need an intermediate model to track which badges a player has earned. We'll call this model Achievements; Example 7-4 gives the code.

Example 7-4. Creating an Achievements model.

```
class CreateAchievements< ActiveRecord::Migration
  def self.up
  create_table :achievements do |t|
  t.integer :user_id
  t.integer :badge_id
  t.timestamps
  end
  end
  def self.down
  drop_table :achievements
  end
end
```

With the achievements table in place, we'll need to add a few lines of code to the models so that Rails understands the relationships between the achievements, badges, and users tables:

```
class Achievement < ActiveRecord::Base
  belongs_to :user
  belongs_to :badge
end
class Badge < ActiveRecord::Base
  has_many :achievements
  ...
class User
  belongs_to :level
  has_many :achievements
  ...
```

With these lines of code in place, Rails knows that each user can have many achievements, and each achievement has a badge. To make awarding badges easier, let's also add a convenience method to the User model:

```
def award_badge(name)
  badge = Badge.find_by_name(name)
  achievements.create(:badge => badge)
end
```

To award a badge, we'll need to make a one-line, readable call, such as user.award_badge("icebreaker"). The method will look up the correct badge, create a new achievement, and log the event in the player's history. Now, all we have to do is write the code to award the badges.

Awarding the First Badge

In Table 7-3, we defined a series of badges. The first is called the Newbie badge, and it is awarded simply for showing up. We already defined an `after_create` method on our User model, so we can expand it to award this badge by adding one line of code to the `award_signup_bonus` method:

```
def award_signup_bonus
  add_points(SIGNUP_BONUS, "Sign-up bonus!")
  award_badge('newbie')
end
```

This revised method will now award a new player her sign-up bonus. We'll then use the `award_badge` method to issue the first player badge.

Subsequent Badge Awards

The next badge, called the Chatterbox, is awarded when a player writes his fifth comment on a post. Since we've already created a callback on the Post model to award points each time a player creates a new post, we can simply expand this code to award the badge:

```
def award_user_points
  user.add_points(POST_BONUS, "You posted a reply.")
  user.award_badge('chatterbox') if user.reload.posts_count == 5
end
```

Here, we've added a new line to the `award_user_points` method to award the Chatterbox badge on the player's fifth post. In most games, a player can lose points but not badges, so we won't code a method to revoke a player's badge if her post is deleted. However, we have created one problem with this new logic. If a player creates five posts, deletes one, and then creates a new fifth post, she will be granted a second Chatterbox badge.

Usually, a player can earn only one of each type of badge. Let's refactor our user#award_badge method slightly to enforce this rule for all badges:

```
def award_badge(name)
  badge = Badge.find_by_name(name)
  unless self.achievements.find_by_badge_id(badge.id)
  self.achievements.create(:badge => badge)
  end
end
```

The revised method will first check to see whether the player already has this badge. It will only award a new achievement if she does not.

The third badge that we defined in Table 7-3 was the Icebreaker badge. This is similar to the Chatterbox badge, but it is awarded when the player creates her third new topic. To do this, we add a line of code to the existing topic#award_user_points method:

```
def award_user_points
 user.add_points(TOPIC_BONUS, "You posted a topic.")
 user.award_badge('icebreaker') if user.topics.count == 3
end
```

This new line works in almost exactly the same as when issuing a Chatterbox badge. The only difference is that Altered Beast keeps a posts_count cache on the User model, but not a topic_count cache, so we have to call the count method on the player's topics in order to calculate when to award the Icebreaker badge.

The final badge we need to implement is the Talk of the Town badge, which the player earns when one of his topics receives 10 posts. Since the trigger for this award will also occur when a new post is saved, we can further expand the post#award_user_points method to award it:

```
def award_user_points
 user.add_points(POST_BONUS, "You posted a reply.")
 user.award_badge('chatterbox') if user.reload.posts_count == 5

 if topic.posts.count(:conditions => ['user_id != ?', topic.user.id]) == 10
 topic.user.award_badge('talk_of_the_town')
 end
end
```

To avoid incentivizing a player to post repeated comments on his own topics just to earn this badge, we don't count a player's own replies toward the award. The topic poster receives a Talk of Town Badge only when his topic gets 10 replies from other players. We've implemented this in a straightforward manner using ActiveRecord's count method, with a condition to filter out the topic creator's posts. When that count equals 10, the topic creator receives the badge.

Now, we have implemented our entire first-pass gamification makeover design. Players get points, move up to higher levels, and earn badges for extraordinary achievements. Taken together, these systems should motivate players to work at becoming high-ranking members of the forums community. To unlock that behavior, though, they'll need to see their rewards—and be able to show them off to their friends. In the next section, we'll walk through displaying this information to a player.

Displaying Player Scores and Levels on the Site

In addition to our internal design, we've given players two powerful outward-facing tools to track their progress on the site: score and level. We've also created an Event model, so players can see how they are earning points. If we want players to find this information meaningful and learn the rules of the community easily, we need to display this information prominently. We'll do this by giving players a status view that contains all their information. We'll also add their current score and level to the header, so they can see it all the time.

Scores and levels are another way for players to show their status to others, so we should also tie their scores and ranks to their public identity on the site. We'll do this by displaying their score and level whenever we display their headshot, such as next to a forum post.

Adding a Player's Score and Level to the Sidebar

To keep the player aware of her point balance, a small score box will appear in the site's righthand column when a player is logged in. As shown in Figure 7-2, the player will now be able to see his score in every view.

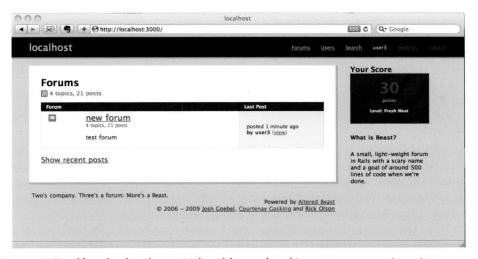

Figure 7-2. By adding the player's score in the sidebar, we keep his awareness on earning points.

We make this happen by adding some display code to the application layout template, *application.html.erb*:

```
<div id="right">
<% if current_user %>
<div id="notice">
<strong>Your Score</strong>
<div id="your_score">
<h3 class="points"><%=current_user.score %></h3>
<h4>points</h4>
<h3 class="level" align="center">
Level: <%=current_user.level.display_name %>
</h3>
</div>
</div>
<% end %>
<%= yield :right %>
</div>
```

We inserted the code snippet in the existing div, just above the yield statement. This ensures that the score box is always at the top of the righthand column, just above any custom notices that might appear in those views. First, we check whether the current_user parameter exists so that our score box will appear only for logged-in players. The next lines format the display of the player's score and current level.

Adding a Player's Level to Topic Posts

Adding the player's current score to the righthand column, as we did above, ensures that he stays aware of his point balance, inspiring him to earn more points. Now, we'll add the player's level to his forum posts. This will associate his rank with his headshot, linking his status and identity on the site.

Altered Beast already marks status by displaying a player's post count, so we can piggyback off that layout. In *views/topics/show.html.erb*, there is a snippet of HTML that writes out the player's post count under her avatar:

```
<span class="posts">
 <%= I18n.t 'txt.count_posts', :count => post.user.posts.size,
 :num => number_with_delimiter(post.user.posts.size) %>
</span>
```

The I18n.t makes use of Rails' internationalization and pluralization features. In this case, if the player has one or two posts and his default language is set to English, it outputs a string such as "1 post" or "2 posts". We'll skip over internationalization for now, and replace the post count with the poster's current level:

```
<span class="level">
 <%=post.user.level.display_name %>
</span>
```

Now, every time a player posts to the forum, her current level appears next to her headshot.

Adding a Basic Leaderboard

 After posting a player's points and level, and printing that current level next to his headshot, his next question will probably be: "Who's winning?" We can answer this question by adding a basic leaderboard to the mix. This is one of the most powerful motivational tools for players who want to increase their scores.

Altered Beast already includes a rudimentary leaderboard. It is a list of all the players on the site, as well as their post count (see Figure 7-3).

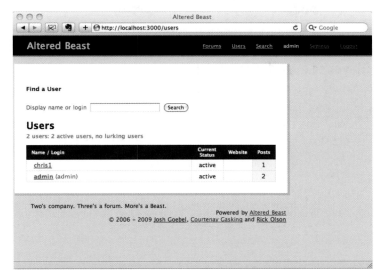

Figure 7-3. The Altered Beast users list already functions as a de facto leaderboard.

This list serves its purpose as a basic directory of players, but we can make it a more powerful tool by turning it into an explicit leaderboard. We'll do this by implementing a few changes, such as:

- Making the first column a score
- Adding a column to display the level as well
- Sorting the table by score so that the highest-scoring players appear at the top of the list

As shown in Figure 7-4, this creates a simple but usable leaderboard, where players can quickly see that the way to the top of the list is by increasing their score.

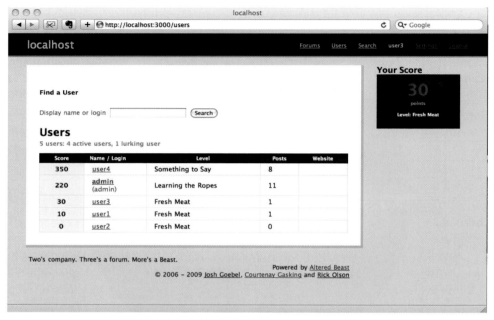

Figure 7-4. Sorting users by score converts the list into a competitive ranking.

Example 7-5 shows the code necessary to transform the players' list into a leader-board. Note the callouts, which highlight where these changes are added to the code. The callouts are explained in the text beneath Example 7-5.

Example 7-5. Turning the user#index view into a leaderboard.

```
      <table border="0" cellspacing="0" cellpadding="0" class="wide forums">
      <tr>
❶    <th>Score</th>
      <th class="la" width="100">
      <%= I18n.t 'txt.views_users.name_or_login', :default => 'Name / Login' %>
      </th>
      <% if logged_in? && current_user.admin? -%>
      <th>
      <%=I18n.t 'txt.views_users.current_status_title',
      :default => "Current Status" %>
      </th>
      <% end -%>
❷    <th width="200">Level</th>
❸    <th><%= I18n.t 'txt.views_users.posts_title', :default => 'Posts' %>
      </th>
      <th><%= I18n.t 'txt.views_users.website_title', :default => 'Website' %></th>
      </tr>
      <% @users.each do |user|-%>
      <tr>
```

```
❹    <td class="ca inv"><strong><%= user.score %></strong></td>
     <td>
     <%=link_to h(user.display_name || user.login), user,
     :class => (user.admin? ? "admin" : nil) %>
     <span style="color:#666">
     <%=I18n.t('txt.views_users.admin_in_parens',
     :default => "(admin)") if user.admin? %>
     </span>
     </td>
     <% if logged_in? && current_user.admin? -%>
     <td><%= user.state %></td>
     <% end -%>
❺    <td><%= user.level.display_name %></td>
     <td><%= user.posts.size %></td>
     <td class="la">
     <% unless user.website.blank? %>
     <%=sanitize link_to(user.website.gsub("http://",""),
     "http://" + user.website.gsub("http://","")) %>
     <% end %>
     </td>
     </tr>
     <% end %>
     </table>
```

❶ *Make Score the first column*
Make Score the first column, and use Altered Beast's `class="la"` tag to make the background gray so the field will stand out.

❷ *Insert a Level column*
Insert the Level column header. Note that we're not using the `I18n.t` method in our columns for simplicity. `I18n.t` is a built-in Rails localization method that looks up display strings depending on the player's locale settings. It's very useful, but it complicates our example.

❸ *Move the Posts column before Website*
Move the Posts column above the Website column, since it relates to Level.

❹ *Insert the player's score*
Within the `@users.each` loop, output the player's score in the first column. We used Altered Beast's `class="ca inv"` CSS to make the column background darker so the score is more visible.

❺ *Insert the player's level*
Output the player's level column.

Optimizing Leaderboard Output

The code in Example 7-5 will output a simple leaderboard of all players, but there is still one problem: the list is not sorted by score, so it's difficult to tell who is winning. This can be fixed with just a few lines of code.

First, we'll need a named scope on the User model. This is a Rails convenience function that lets you define search criteria—in this case, a sort order—for a model, and give it a clear name. We do this by adding a line to the User model:

```
named_scope :by_score, :order => 'score DESC'
```

This code tells Rails: "When I specify a search by_score, order the results by score, in descending order." To use it for our leaderboard, we need to modify the line of code in the UsersController#index method that sends the list of players to the view. The current method loads a paginated array of all players for the current site:

```
@users = current_site.send(users_scope).paginate(:page => current_page)
```

In essence, the method asks the current site to return a list of players without specifying a sort order. The .paginate() method is a handy Rails extension that handles breaking the list into manageable chunks that the view can use for display. To sort the array, we can use our new score-sorting scope:

```
@users = current_site.send(users_scope).by_score.paginate(:page => current_page)
```

We inserted the by_score scope at the end of the array method, just before paginating it. Now, the line of code returns an array of players for the current site, sorted by score and paginated for the current view's page.

Easy Leaderboard Enhancements

Now, we have a fully functional (if not very dynamic) leaderboard. There are a number of ways that we could enhance the leaderboard to increase its appeal. A few simple extensions would be to:

- Add headshots to clearly connect player identity and status
- Include an explicitly numbered rank so that players can more easily see the top 10, 25, 50, and so on
- Add sorting so that players can change the rank order by score, level, or number of postings
- Rename the view to explicitly define it as a leaderboard in the top navigation

Next, we'll give players a special place to show off all the points and status they've earned: a trophy case.

The Trophy Case

Winning something such as a badge or other achievement is much less meaningful if your peers don't know of your accomplishment. The easiest way to convey this is to create a trophy case or trophy room—the detailed display of the player's rank and achievements. In a more advanced design, with badges and virtual items, this would be the place to show the entire array of player achievements in one spot, accessible to all players.

Altered Beast already includes a simple player display, accessible from the leaderboard. If you click on a player's name, you'll see a page such as the one shown in Figure 7-5.

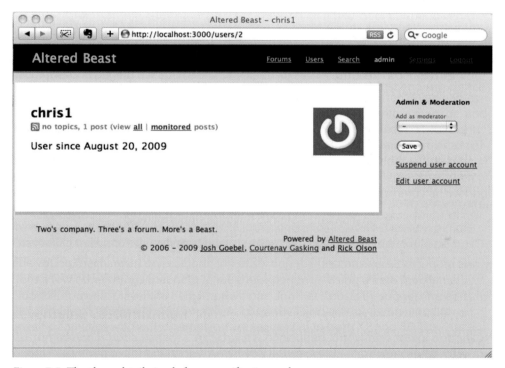

Figure 7-5. The player detail view before a gamification makeover.

The current view is all business. It displays the player's name, headshot, and posting count, but it's not very interesting beyond that. We can enhance it by adding the player's score, level, and recent history so that it looks more like Figure 7-6.

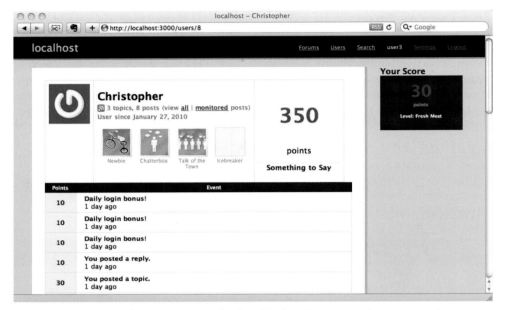

Figure 7-6. By prominently featuring points, level, and badges, the user view becomes a trophy case.

To do this, we need to modify the user display view, which is located in *views/users/show.html.erb*. By including players' achievements, we'll turn the view into a simple trophy case. Before we implement the view, however, there is a way we can make it more powerful.

Listing the Badges That a Player Has Not Yet Earned

Because badges award special achievements, they can be powerful motivators for players. But in order to fully unlock that power, players might want to know some or all of the available badges. One easy way to convey that information is to show a list of grayed-out badges that the player has yet to earn. To provide that list, we can add a convenience method to the User model:

```
def unearned_badges
  if self.achievements.nil?
  unearned_badges = Badge.find(:all)
  else
  unearned_badges = []
  Badge.find(:all).each do |badge|
  unearned_badges << badge unless self.achievements.find_by_badge_id(badge.id)
  end
  end
  unearned_badges
end
```

The method first checks a player's achievements. If there aren't any, it will return all possible badges. Otherwise, the method loops through each possible badge, adding it to a hash if the player has not already earned it. The method then returns the hash of badges the player hasn't earned, which we can use in the trophy case to display all badges, earned and unearned. See the full code listing in Example 7-6.

Example 7-6. Adding a trophy case to the user view.

```
...
<table cellspacing="0" cellpadding="5" border="0">
<tr>
<td width="80" valign="top"><%= avatar_for @user, 80 %></td>
❶  <td valign="top">
<h1><%=h @user.display_name %></h1>
<p class="subtitle">
<%= feed_icon_tag @user.display_name,
user_posts_path(:user_id => @user, :format => :rss) %>
<span>
<%=I18n.t 'txt.count_topics', :count => @user.topics.size,
:num => number_with_delimiter(@user.topics.size) %>,
<%=I18n.t 'txt.count_posts', :count => @user.posts.size,
:num => number_with_delimiter(@user.posts.size) %>
(<%= I18n.t 'txt.view', :default => 'view' %>
<%= link_to I18n.t('txt.all', :default => 'all'),
user_posts_path(@user) %> |
<%= link_to I18n.t('txt.monitored', :default => 'monitored'), "#" %>
<%= I18n.t 'txt.posts', :default => 'posts' %>)
<br/>
</span>
</p>
<%= @user.bio_html %>
<% unless @user.website.blank? -%>
<p><strong><%= I18n.t 'txt.website', :default => 'Website' %></strong>
<%= sanitize link_to(@user.website.gsub("http://",""),
"http://" + @user.website.gsub("http://","")) %>
<% end -%>
<p class="subtitle">
<%= I18n.t 'txt.user_since', :default => 'User since {{date}}',
:date => @user.created_at.to_date.to_s(:long) %></p>
❷  <% @user.achievements.each do |achievement| %>
<div class="badge">
<%= image_tag("badges/#{achievement.badge.name}.jpg") %>
<span><%= achievement.badge.display_name %></span>
</div>
<% end %>
❸  <% @user.unearned_badges.each do |badge| %>
<div class="badge">
<%= image_tag('badges/unearned.jpg') %>
<span><%= badge.display_name %></span>
</div>
<% end %>
</td>
<td width="160" valign="top" align="center">
```

```
❹    <p id="user_score"><%=@user.score %></p>
     <p>points</p>
❺    <p id="user_level"><%=@user.level.display_name %></p>
     </td>
     </tr>
     </table>
     <table border="0" cellspacing="0" cellpadding="0" class="wide forums">
     <tr>
     <th width="40">Points</th>
     <th>Event</th>
     </tr>
❻    <% @user.events.each do |event|-%>
     <tr>
     <td class="ca inv"><strong><%= event.points %></strong></td>
     <td>
     <strong><%= event.text %></strong>
     <br/>
     <%= distance_of_time_in_words_to_now(event.created_at) %> ago
     </td>
     </tr>
     <% end %>
     </table>
```

❶ *Change table alignment*
  Change the table alignment to "top" so that badges line up properly

❷ *Display earned achievements*
  Loop through player's achievements and display the badges won

❸ *Display unearned achievements*
  Use the unearned_badges method to display badges that can still be won

❹ *Display score*
  Add the player's score to the view

❺ *Display level*
  Add the player's current level to the view

❻ *Display recent activity*
  Loop through the player's logged events

The view code in Example 7-6 shows the changes we made to the existing user detail view. The view now loops through the player's badges and outputs each badge image and display name. Then, it loops through the badges the player has not yet earned, retrieving them from the User#unearned_badges method we created earlier. We've also added a prominent display of the player's current points and score.

The last section of Example 7-6 sets up a table, and then loops through the player events table to display the player's point history. That lays out all of the game play information we want the players to see, and it should serve to focus their attention on trying to earn more badges, points, and higher levels.

Summary

In this chapter, we've covered the basics for applying simple gamification in a forums site. You've seen examples of how to implement the core backend elements of game mechanics: tracking scores, measuring levels, and awarding points. You've also seen some examples of how to design and utilize key awards to motivate players, such as sign-up, login, and activity bonuses. In addition, we've illustrated basic implementations of key views, such as displaying an "always on" dashboard score, adding the level to a player's site identity, providing a leaderboard, and displaying a trophy case.

Clearly, this is not the limit of game design for basic websites. The range of options to incentivize and direct player behavior is limited only by your imagination—but these basics form a critical foundation for moving to the next level.

In the next chapter, we'll look at another approach. With Badgeville, an off-the-shelf gamification solution, we'll use simple APIs to implement sophisticated game mechanics without having to code everything by hand.

CHAPTER 8

Tutorial: Using an Instant Gamification Platform

In Chapter 7, we walked through the implementation of a basic game layer, coding out all the pieces by hand. Another approach, which can help you get started more quickly, is to use a gamification platform like Badgeville.

Badgeville (*http://badgeville.com*) is a white label social-rewards and analytics platform, and is sponsoring this chapter. Along with a sophisticated analytics engine to help tune your implementation, Badgeville has a suite of tools to help website and mobile app developers leverage game mechanics to integrate users in an immersive social experience,

In this chapter, we'll walk you through how to use Badgeville, and how to employ game mechanics and loyalty best practices to influence player behavior, grow their loyalty, and make your site or app successful.

Game On

Using game mechanics to build rewards and loyalty programs can help turn visitors into fans, and fans into advocates. The games need not be elaborate or overt. For example, you can start with leaderboards that feature top members of the week. Or, you can use real-time notification of award achievements, and display them in a strategic location to provide an inviting hum of participation. The overarching premise is simple: you define the important interactions on your site, and then reward players when they participate or compete to perform those actions. When you're ready, you can add layers of more advanced reward-based interactions.

A well-implemented rewards program should serve to convert simple user IDs into players who actively help you understand what's good about your site or app—and what's not. Next-generation analytics isn't based on page views, it's built using an engaging layer of people playing, enjoying, and sharing their experiences.

Critical Elements of an Online Rewards Experience

A social-rewards program grows loyalty by making a significant behavior-changing connection with the player. Several key elements increase your chance of making this connection. An effective online rewards experience must be contextual, use real-time feedback, leverage the social web, and be a vehicle for accomplishment.

Relevant context is important because visitors and members have unconsciously and consciously trained themselves to ignore information that isn't interesting or relevant to them. A better gamification platform will allow you to learn about your users and then customize their online experience based on their actions and interests.

The necessity of real-time feedback is obvious: a player enjoys and appreciates instant gratification. But, more importantly, real-time status updates give her confidence—she knows where she is and where's she's going. And when she can share achievement with her friends and get kudos from her network, the experience is even more powerful.

From a publisher's (e.g., site owner, app developer, or content creator) perspective, social-sharing is a powerful marketing tool. Understanding that 30% of Foursquare badges are shared into Facebook, and that the average Facebook user has 150 friends, social-sharing features are too useful to ignore.

An online rewards program can be a source of continued achievement because it offers a multitude of accomplishments of varying degrees of difficulty. While a player may not explicitly recognize micro achievements as a source of deep satisfaction, they are. The overwhelming success of apps like *FarmVille* is an example of this.

In the next section, we'll walk you through the design and implementation of Skumo, a mock site for finding local businesses (see Figure 8-1). Members review businesses and comment on those reviews.

Planning a Rewards Project

Gamifying a complete social rewards project requires an implementation plan that includes many tasks. For simplicity, we'll break it down into two domains: design and development. Here are a few key areas we'll cover:

Design

- Selecting business objectives
- Defining desired behaviors and metadata
- Designing games (to achieve the objectives)
- Defining levels
- Defining rewards, achievements, and badges

Development

- Creating your rewards program in the Publisher module
- Preparing methods to call the API
- Preparing methods to parse JSON data
- Registering and tracking players
- Enabling behavior tracking
- Configuring widgets (leaderboards, profiles, activity)
- Creating a rewards notification
- (Optional) Integrating Badgeville with third-party systems, such as a commenting system

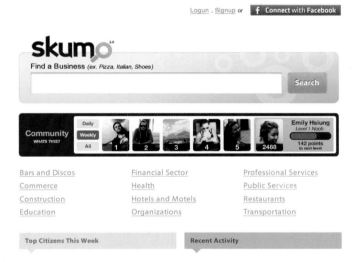

Figure 8-1. The Skumo home page.

Selecting Business Objectives

In order to drive the most success, begin the project by understanding its business objectives. What important business problem do you want to solve? A successful rewards program supports your ability to achieve core business objectives. Some common examples of appropriate objectives for a rewards program include:

- Increasing ad revenue
- Increasing sponsorship revenue
- Reducing content-creation costs
- Reducing content-moderation costs

Skumo's objectives

Skumo's main objective is to increase ad and sponsorship revenue by providing useful content that grows membership. As a business, Skumo cannot afford to hire full-time writers and editors, so it uses technology to drive a creation and moderation process that elevates useful content. Skumo's challenge is universal for web publishers: how do you reduce costs while improving product quality? The answer: tell your members what you need, make it fun for them to participate, and reward them for doing so.

Defining Desired Behaviors

Behaviors are the actions that players perform that help achieve your objectives, such as registering or reading articles. You should select a few behaviors to implement for an initial launch. Here are a few examples of behaviors that support common publisher objectives:

- Signing in
- Visiting a page
- Sharing a page
- Uploading a photo or video
- Buying a product
- Making a payment
- Voting or participating in a survey
- Providing feedback
- Participating in promotions

For each behavior, you'll identify the metadata you want to use as the basis for rewards and analysis. For example, for reading pages, you'll probably collect information like category, topic, and author so you can make relevant rewards and targeted activity or leaderboard widgets.

Skumo is successful to the degree that members add reviews, comments, and ratings, and share the content outside the site. Thus, Skumo promotes and tracks these behaviors:

- Adding, rating, and reading reviews
- Adding, rating, and reading comments
- Promoting content
- Becoming a member

Because Skumo has a natural taxonomy based on industries, this data can be used to reward users who view specific types of reviews, like restaurants. These behaviors are discussed later in this chapter.

Designing the Games

Once you understand the business objectives and the relevant behaviors, you can define games to achieve them. Games don't have to be complex, but they need to have either defined or implied winning conditions—for example, getting more points in a week than a friend, or achieving an enviable status.

To target specific player types, game techniques can be paired with several types of motivators: personal, friend, and group. See Figure 8-2 for an example.

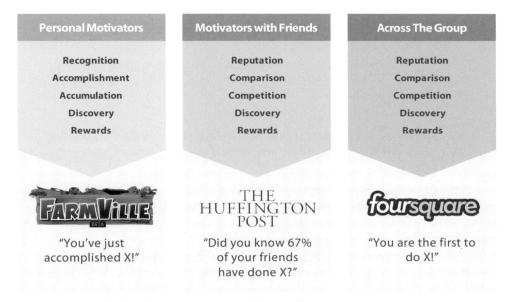

Figure 8-2. Personal, friend, and group motivators leveraged by game designers.

Personal motivators resonate with an individual because they satisfy core needs for achievement and recognition. For some players, accumulation is a powerful motivator because it can be a vehicle for self-expression: what you own may reflect who you are. For others, collecting rewards feels like being on a treasure hunt—they feel richer for the experience.

Friends provide an incredibly rich domain of motivators that can increase game design success. People greatly value the opinion of their friends, but they are also much more comfortable competing with and bragging to their friends. Thus, a rewards program that leverages reputation, comparison, competition, and discovery among friends will be more likely to succeed.

Similar to friend-based motivators, you can use group-based motivators to engage your players effectively. People like to stand out in a crowd and be known. They also enjoy comparing themselves with and competing against an anonymous crowd. Social games have used these motivators successfully for years. You should use them in your rewards programming design to increase participation and build a more loyal fan base.

Skumo design

Based on our business objectives, we identified several player types:

Reviewers
> These players respond to personal, friend, and group motivators. They want to become a site celebrity. Thus, they want more than just the sense of belonging—they want recognition.

Commenters
> These players are like reviewers, but they may not have the time or ambition to craft useful reviews; they do, however, want recognition.

Raters
> At the other end of the spectrum, raters want to be useful and want to contribute, but they are not motivated to be known in the group.

Obviously, any single player can respond to multiple types of motivation, but we use the distinctions to inform game design. For example, we'll promote reviewer profiles more actively on the site. We'll be sure to make comparisons of commenters' achievements wherever we expose friend rewards in a user profile. For raters, we'll make progress toward level improvement prominent. (Raters are driven by helping, so we want to make progress and accomplishment very visible.)

Using this understanding of player roles and motivations, as well as our business objectives, we can make simple games. For example, we can make a game, *Sage Reviewer*, that drives players to create the most reviews in a given week. Winners are featured in a leaderboard and highlighted in special areas on the site. Similarly, we can provide a weekly game that rewards comment creation. Top commenters are featured in a dedicated leaderboard but will not be featured personalities on the site. To ensure reviews and comments are high quality, we can provide the *Roaring Rater* game, in which members are rewarded weekly for rating reviews and comments. The cost of participating in *Roaring Rating* is low, but the value returned to the site is high. Members easily accomplish useful tasks and gain rewards and status.

Beyond these core games, there are games you provide because the additional cost of doing so is nominal and the return is too great to ignore:

Power Promoter

> Become a top promoter by sharing reviews and comments. Played weekly and ongoing, this game is driven by rewards, such as badges.

Model Member

> Become a model member by rating reviews, comments, and businesses. Played weekly and ongoing, this game is driven by status, represented by levels.

Defining Levels

Levels define status on your site. While many factors inform level design, you can start by considering two factors: site theme and anticipated usage.

Your theme will provide a rich domain of naming choices. If you run a site for horticulturists, for example, your first level may be seedling. It's crucial to remember that levels define status, and unless membership itself is exclusive, you want members to earn enviable status. Thus, lower levels denote potential, and higher levels represent achievement and respectability. For sites that leverage humor, lower-level names may be based on objects of ridicule, such as "noob" (i.e., newbie). You have to choose wisely though, because most people are not incentivized by insults. For a gadget site, new members can start as newbies and grow to become gurus. These levels have a fundamental and powerful meaning to such an audience. Few members of a gadget community want to be known as a newbie, so players will likely strive to advance.

Unless you've done some analytics, you may not have a good idea of the usage profile of your average player. However, you could deploy Badgeville in tracking mode to study the usage of your site. For this exercise, we'll ask some basic questions to make educated guesses. How many times does a member visit per day? How many pages does he read? Estimate site usage for your ideal average player, then break it down into times per day he performs the behavior. For example, the average player visits once per day, reads five articles, and makes one comment.

Next, assign relative point value to each behavior. With Skumo, for example, the most significant player behavior is creating reviews, which is twice as important as commenting. This is because creating reviews takes longer and can provide many SEO opportunities for your site. Commenting, on the other hand, takes less time. That said, readers value comments highly, as they can understand by the writing whether the reviewer is reasonable and has similar values. Thus, we can state that reviews are worth 50 points, comments are worth 25 points, and ratings are worth 10 points. Behaviors that require less effort but still provide value are rewarded but are worth less. For example, site visits are five points and reading pages are five as well. In this system, it's not enough to show up—you have to play.

Based on these estimates, let's create a simple table:

Behavior	Times	Points	Daily value
Visit	1	5	5
Read	10	5	50
Review	0	50	0
Comment	1	25	25
Rate	3	10	30
		Daily total	110
		Yearly total	5720

Remember that in environments such as games and websites, participation is rarely a bell curve. Thus, your level design should recognize that the power law of distribution (e.g., the 80/20 rule of active users to passive users) is probably more relevant in anticipating possible usage. You don't have to solve for this problem, but you should be aware of it.

Level design recommendations

To design levels effectively using the Badgeville system, it's useful to consider a few design concepts that you can add to the strategies described earlier in this book:

- Create a profile of a common player and the actions she performs daily. Multiply that by 365 to get a rough idea of her accumulated points for a year.

- To provide immediate satisfaction and reward for new players, create a level they earn upon registering for your site.

- Make the first few levels easier to attain to incentivize players to participate more often.

- Start with three or four levels and monitor usage. Use analytics to design higher levels.

- While Badgeville lets you redefine levels, it is recommended that you avoid restructuring levels so that users are not demoted.

Skumo level design

Below is an example table that contains starting levels based on our anticipated usage calculations, as well as our understanding of Skumo membership. The leveling theme is "hometown" because the site promotes local businesses; so, we use the concept of citizenship to name the levels.

The first level is Tourist. While it is certainly fun to be a tourist, it's rarely a compliment (that said, it's not offensive). If you do stay for a while, you can become an Expat (expatriate)—a long-time resident but still not a full citizen. A Citizen is someone who belongs but isn't necessarily respected. A Model Citizen belongs and is respected.

These starting levels can take Skumo through a year or so until further levels are needed. This approach can be extended by defining more value-laden names, or simply by adding numeric levels, Model Citizen 1, etc.:

Level name	Point range
Model Citizen	12,000–24,999
Citizen	4,000–11,999
Expat	1,000–3,999
Tourist	0–999

Trophies

Trophies represent levels visually, but more importantly, they represent status and reputation within your community. Using your site theme to inspire the design, make trophies that indicate rank clearly. You can display trophies in player profiles, leaderboards, or wherever rank is used to educate and engage.

As shown in Figure 8-3, Skumo's first level is depicted as a camera, which is commonly associated with tourists. Next, Expat is shown as a passport. Citizen is represented by green crown of leaves, which is an iconic image associated with democracy. Finally, Model Citizen is depicted as a golden crown.

Figure 8-3. Skumo trophies.

Defining Rewards, Achievements, and Badges

You reward achievements on your site with virtual goods, such as badges, trophies, and points. Rewards can also be tangible, like coupons, discounts, or early access to premium content and features. Points or virtual currency can be used as rewards, too.

Skumo's short-term rewards strategy relies on low-cost virtual rewards, such as attractive badges, and then later supports tangible rewards, like discounts or coupons sponsored by reviewed businesses. We'll share some basic thinking around reward and badge design, and then show you a sample badge collection for Skumo.

Badge design

When designing badges, you should consider several factors, including aesthetics, psychology, and icons. Visually, badges should be works of art. If badges were clothing, they are what you would wear to look your best. While badges do not cost anything, they aren't free—players have to earn them. As such, badges represent effort and accomplishment.

Most people enjoy defining or expressing themselves through achievement and acquisition. From the clothes they wear to the cars they drive, people surround themselves with goods that reflect their personalities and status. Our virtual selves are no different.

Note. *Unlike icons, badges can be displayed at various sizes. Your design should be flexible to accommodate this. Also, locked badges can be shown in grayscale with a lock overlaid. You should consider these cases when designing badges.*

Reward collections

A collection is a group of rewards that encourages a single behavior. Most rewards programs use two collection types: ladder and prize. You use the ladder type to reward a player with an ever-increasing, more desirable reward for one specific ongoing behavior, such as visiting the site. Ladder rewards (shown in Figure 8-4) leverage personal and friend motivators as they support personal achievement, recognition, and comparison. You use the prize badge type to reward one-time actions, such as enabling Facebook-sharing or participating in a promotion.

Bronze Coin	Silver Coin	Gold Coin	Bag of Gold	Gemstones	Jeweled Crown	Treasure Chest
1st visit	2nd visit	5th visit	10th visit	25th visit	50th visit	100th visit
New York City	Los Angeles	London	Paris	Rome	Tokyo	Milan

Figure 8-4. Examples of ladder collections that encourage repeat visits to gaming- and fashion-themed sites.

Example rewards structure

Skumo uses the rewards structure shown in the table below. You can use a similar table to define your site's structure:

Behavior	Badge type	Triggers
Visits	Ladder	Seven stages For visits: 1, 2, 5, 10, 25, 50, 100
Reading	Ladder	Seven stages For reading pages: 10, 25, 50, 100, 250, 500, 1,000
Rating	Ladder	Five stages For rating: 1, 5, 10, 25, 50
Commenting	Ladder	Five stages For comments: 1, 5, 10, 25, 50

Badge Design Recommendations

- Invest in good badge design because badges are works of art.
- Use the language of your community.
- Use color progression consistently across badge collections—for example, make starter badges bluish and advanced badges reddish.
- Use numeric values on badges when image alone does not convey value.

Rewards UX Design

Your investment in social rewards is wasted if they're buried at the bottom of your pages. We recommend displaying the rewards platform as prominently as possible—without making it obtrusive. There are many places you can surface rewards data and interactions without losing valuable screen real estate. We'll show examples of the following components and how they can be used:

- Login header
- Leaderboard
- User profile
- Rewards notification
- Inline with content

Login header

You can use a login header to display a logged in player's current level and status. To conserve space, only display information such as a progress bar and points total, enticing the player to further explore the control. For example, hovering over the progress bar displays the player's rewards summary, and clicking the profile image or name opens the player's profile page (see Figure 8-5).

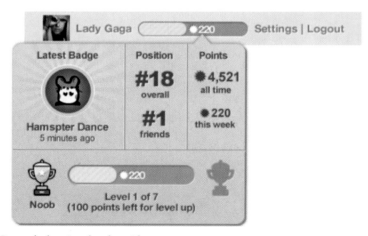

Figure 8-5. Rewards data in a header widget.

Leaderboard

A leaderboard displays your site's top fans for a given time period. It is one of the most important tools for educating and encouraging your players. Social yet competitive, a leaderboard is the public space where members are recognized and rewarded for loyal participation. Using the rich metadata you captured with user behaviors, you can create contextual leaderboards. For example, you can show the most active members who read stories in a specific category, or showcase valued members who help make areas on your site successful. You can include a leaderboard almost anywhere—you can embed longer leaderboards in sidebars (as shown in Figure 8-6), or shorter ones in content templates.

Figure 8-6. A complete leaderboard for a sidebar.

User profile

A user profile is a critical component to an awards program. Where a leaderboard is a social scoreboard, a user profile can be a personal scoreboard that features accomplishments and provides guidance about next steps. A user profile should also support achievement-sharing. You can design a profile UI that fits into a tab on a leaderboard or is a complete page, as shown in Figure 8-7.

Figure 8-7. User profile that includes shareable rewards.

Rewards notification

Displaying rewards in real time is important, but not annoying your players is also critical. More and more sites are using the bottom of the screen to communicate updates to players. You can use this area to reward players in a subtle but effective way. The rewards notification design can also include social-sharing features, and provide access to a player's profile or account settings. See Figure 8-8.

Figure 8-8. Real-time notification of awards.

Inline with content

You can surface rewards content just about anywhere; for example, Philly.com embeds a comment microwidget in its commenting system, as shown in Figure 8-9. Player level, trophies, and points appear inside the player information portion of the comment UI.

Emily Hsiung 🏆 **LEVEL 6 SUPERSTAR**
THIS is what they decided would be good to do with the brand??? Wow.
Posted 2:27 PM, 02/16/2011

l.jenkins 🏆 **LEVEL 1 NOOB**
They were in bankruptcy. the purpose of bankruptcy is to satisfy the creditors, not to do what is good for the brand. The brand was already done.
Posted 2:49 PM, 02/16/2011

dunsmore 🏆 **LEVEL 5 STAR**
No more selling outside of the US then either? They're just going to take away their Canadian markets just like that too?
Posted 3:27 PM, 02/16/2011

go_matt 🏆 **LEVEL 5 STAR**
The place needs to do something, that's for sure.
Posted 3:34 PM, 02/16/2011

furn800 🏆 **LEVEL 2 GUEST**
These companies need to pick 1 market or the other. You can either market your brand as exclusive, limited quantities, well constructed etc or you can market them as low - mid range clothing and forget about tapping the high end market
Posted 4:11 PM, 02/16/2011

Figure 8-9. Embedding rewards comment inline with other content.

Leveraging Your Theme

Your site probably has a theme that you can use to inspire your games and rewards. For example, a gaming site may use treasure as the basis for rewards. A first visit may receive a bronze coin badge, but the 50th visit may earn a jeweled crown badge. A theme is not required, but it certainly helps all facets of game and reward design.

Skumo uses the badge collection shown in Figure 8-10 to reward commenting. The badges get more intricate and the explicit value increases.

| First comment | 5th comment | 10th comment | 25th comment | 50th comment |

Figure 8-10. Skumo comment badges.

Developing a Rewards Program

You can implement a Badgeville rewards program by using their Plug and Play widgets. Or, you can integrate your rewards and loyalty programs deeply into your website or application using Badgeville's API. This section walks you through the development of Skumo, which mostly uses the Badgeville API.

Code Examples in This Chapter

Badgeville provides a RESTful API that returns data in JSON format. Thus, you can use just about any language to query the API. We provide Ruby samples taken from Skumo.

Step 1: Creating a Rewards Program in the Publisher Module

Badgeville provides a Publisher module, shown in Figure 8-11, that allows you to create and monitor all the system objects you need to provide a rewards and loyalty program. You define business objectives, reputation levels, rewards, business rules for awards, and more. Create the rewards programs you reference in your code before running the code.

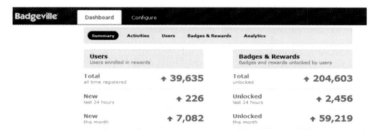

Figure 8-11. Badgeville's Publisher module enables you to control and monitor your system objects.

Before you begin developing, you should create at least one level, a business rule, and a reward (see Figure 8-12). The following steps explain how to create a reward:

1. In the Publisher module, navigate to Configure→Rewards→Simple.

2. Click Create New. The Reward editor appears.

3. Enter a reward name.

4. Enter a description, which appears in the notification when a player earns the reward.

5. Select a behavior (if the reward is associated with a behavior).

6. Select one or more business rules that apply.

7. Click Save.

Figure 8-12. Creating business rules for awards.

Once you save a reward, it's available in the system. Once you activate a reward, it's available in the system. Badgeville also provides advanced features that allow you to define the behavior and metadata to be collected when a user performs the behavior. For brevity, we won't create all required reward objects; instead, we'll move on to discussing project coding.

Step 2: Calling the API

You can make a method to call the API and assign the JSON data to a variable or object. The method accepts a URL argument. Skumo uses the following code to handle calls to the Badgeville API:

```
def bv_send_request(api_url)
 url = URI.parse(URI.escape(api_url))
 req = Net::HTTP::Get.new("#{url.path}?#{url.query}")
 res = Net::HTTP.start(url.host, url.port) { |http| http.request(req) }
 return JSON.parse(res.body)
end
```

We make a generic method that receives a URL, cleans up the URL, makes an HTTP request to the target defined in the URL, and returns data in JSON format (a light-weight data format that is widely adopted due to its ease of use and native browser support). Since we use Ruby, we can either use the standard URI library, or a Ruby gem that handles URLs. You can easily create your own variation of a generic URL handler that prepares the URL to make a request, sends the request, and receives JSON data. Most modern languages have built-in support for JSON.

Here are some commonly used URL endpoints :

Register an activity
> http://**badgeville_host**/api/**publisher_id**/users/**user_session**/
> user_badges?behavior=**behavior**

Retrieve top fans for a week (to display in a leaderboard)
> http:// **badgeville_host**/api/**publisher_id** /users/week_top_fans

Retrieve user-specific data to display in a user profile
> http://**badgeville_host**/api/**publisher_id** /users/**user_session**

Retrieve the next badge for a specific user
> http://**badgeville_host**/api/**publisher_id**/users/**user_session**>/user_badges/
> next?behavior=**behavior**

Step 3: Parsing JSON Data

The Badgeville API returns data in JSON format, so you must create a method to parse data returned from the Badgeville server to extract the information you need. The structure of the JSON data depends on the endpoint you call. For example, this is the call for the leader board:

```
url = http://badgeville_host/api/publisher_id/users/week_top_fans
json = bv_send_request(url)
@bv_users = json["top_users"] if json["result"]
```

In this example, we pass the week_top_fans endpoint as a URL to the method we made earlier (bv_send_request), and assign the returned JSON data to a variable. When we make the assignment, we confirm that there is a result. If we have data, we take the top_users array in the JSON data and store it in the array @bv_users.

Step 4: Register and Track Players

Before you can track and thus reward player behaviors, you must be able to identify them. You can use a JavaScript-based tracker that Badgeville provides, or make calls to the API directly. Skumo tracks behaviors of registered players by calling the API, as shown in the next section, "Step 5: Enabling a Behavior on Your Site."

To track activity for a specific player, you do not have to integrate Badgeville with your user authentication system. Simply create a method that passes existing player information, such as an email and display name, to the Badgeville update_info endpoint. Here is a Ruby example that registers a player:

```
def send_information_to_badgeville(user)
  url = "http://badgeville_host/api/publisher_id/users/update_info"
  url << "?email=#{user.email}&display_name=#{user.name}"
  return bv_send_request(url)
end
```

In this example, we use the method we made earlier, bv_send_request, to register and update players. The URL we pass contains information that Badgeville uses for identification and notification purposes. While authentication is handled by your existing system, Badgeville provides additional player validation to ensure the request is legitimate. The update_info endpoint returns a Badgeville user session ID, which you use in subsequent calls to the API to get user-specific data. Here is the code that assigns the value of the session ID to a variable, bv_session:

```
...
obj = send_information_to_badgeville(@user)
session["bv_session"] = obj["session"] if session["result"]
...
```

When you call the method above, you capture the player's Badgeville session ID from a library that is loaded when he logs in. This code uses the send_information_to_badgeville method to pass the user object to Badgeville and receive a user session ID.

Step 5: Enabling a Behavior on Your Site

Once you know who the current player is, you can enable behavior tracking by either using a Badgeville JavaScript function or by calling the API to register activity. Skumo tracks review creation, commenting, rating, and other player activities using the API. To do this, you define methods that are called from within your code when necessary; for example, when a player submits a review or adds a comment to a review.

Here is sample code for capturing pages read in the politics category:

```
def send_rateComment
 url = "http://badgeville_host/api/publisher_id/users/#{session["bv_session"]}"
 url << "/activities/new?behavior=RateComment&category=politics"
 url << "&url=#{request.url}"))
 resp = bv_send_request(url)
 @badges = resp["badges"] || []
end
```

In this example, you again pass a URL to the bv_send_request method, but the URL is a specific endpoint. In this case, it's the endpoint for rating a comment. You can create one behavior to track all ratings, or individual behaviors to track and reward content-specific ratings.

Here is sample code for capturing a visit:

```
def send_visit
 url = "http://badgeville_host/api/publisher_id/users/#{session["bv_session"]}"
 url << /activities/new?behavior=Visit&url=#{request.url}"))
 resp = bv_send_request(url)
 @badges = resp["badges"] || []
end
...
```

When you register an activity, Badgeville returns a success message in JSON format that includes any badges the player unlocked. Real-time notification of achievements is critical. Instant gratification is a powerful motivator for most players.

Antigaming Logic

Badgeville supports antigaming in many ways, but for generic behaviors, you can define a cool-down period for behavior registration. You can set the length of time that must elapse before a player can get credit for a behavior again.

While most players won't try to game the system, your design must recognize that some will do so. So, to protect the integrity of the system, you need to maximize antigaming.

Step 6: Creating a Leaderboard

Skumo displays a leaderboard on its home page. An out-of-the-box Badgeville leaderboard widget contains three tabs: a site leaderboard, a friends tab (with a leaderboard listing a player's friends), and a user profile. This widget leverages the motivators discussed previously to encourage and motivate all types of members.

Displaying the leaderboard

After calling the Leaderboard endpoint, you can display Leaderboard data. To do so, iterate over the players in the JSON object and pull relevant data for each player:

```
<div>
<h2>Top Citizens This Week </h2>
<ul style="list-style-type: none;">
<% @bv_users.each do |user| %>
<li style="float: left; margin-top: 15px; margin-right: 15px;">
<h3 style="font-size: 50px; float: left; margin-right: 5px;">
<%= user["leaderboard_position"] %> </h3>
<img style="width:64px;height:64px;" src=" <%= user["picture"] %> " alt="" />
<p> <%= user["display_name"] %> </p>
<p> <%= user["week_points"] %> week points</p>
</li>
<% end %>
</ul>
</div>
```

The code above uses Ruby to demonstrate a simple version of a leaderboard that displays players by weekly point totals.

Step 7: Creating a User Profile

After calling the user profile endpoint, you can display user profile data. You can show a user profile that lists the badges the player unlocked, as well as her point total and current level:

```
<% if @bv_user %>
    <div style="text-align: center;">
            <h2>Badgeville</h2><br/>
            <img style="width:64px;height:64px;margin:0px 25px"
src="<%= @bv_user["picture"] %>" alt ="" />
<img src="<%= @bv_user["level_picture"] %>" alt ="" />
<span><%= @bv_user["display_name"] %></span><br/>
<span><%= @bv_user["level"] %></span><br/><br/>
<span><%= @bv_user["total_badges"] %> Badges</span><br/>
<span><%= @bv_user["points"] %> Points</span><br/>
<br/>
</div>
<%end%>
```

Using Ruby, the code above shows a simple version of a user profile that displays basic information.

Example: BeatTheGMAT.com

BeatTheGMAT is the world's largest social network for MBA applicants, serving over 2 million people each year. Their mission is to be the top community that empowers people to learn, share, teach, and support each other throughout the MBA admissions process. BeatTheGMAT is leveraging game mechanics in many powerful ways to add additional value to their extensive knowledge base (see Figure 8-13). For example, they made a game of content tagging to repurpose useful articles. They are leveraging reputation in important locations, like within the forum system.

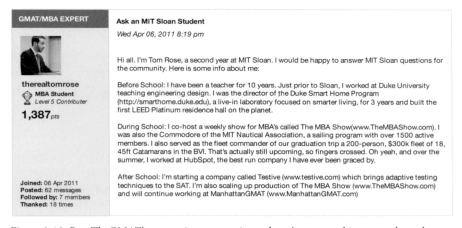

Figure 8-13. BeatTheGMAT's reputation system ties a player's status to his avatar throughout the site.

Step 8: Displaying Rewards

It's important to display rewards in real time. With an activity request, if the player unlocks a badge, the badge information is returned in the response from Badgeville. You assign badges to a variable to show the notification to the player. Here is an example of notification display:

 Note. *This example assumes you have a DIV for badge display defined in your template.*

```
<% if !@badges.blank? %>
 <% @badges.each do |user_badge| -%>
  <% if user_badge["level"].blank? %>
  <div class="badge">
   <img src="<%= user_badge["badge"]["image"] %>"/>
   <p><%=h user_badge["badge"]["name"] %></p>
  </div>
 <% else %>
  <div class="badge">
   <img src="<%= user_badge["level"]["trophy_image"] %>"/>
   <p><%=h user_badge["level"]["name"] %></p>
  </div>
  <% end %>
 <br class="clear" />
 <% end %>
 <% end -%>
```

This code example does not contain all the text from the notification widget—just the code to display the rewards data. If your platform can pass data to the JavaScript layer, you can use the `Badgeville.toast` function in the Badgeville JavaScript API to display rewards and avoid writing your own custom display widget.

Skumo notifies players when they unlock achievements by displaying a simulated pop-up window in the lower-right corner of the browser.

Step 9: Creating an Activities Widget

An Activities widget is the pulse of your rewards community. It advertises player achievements, inviting and educating your players on what they can do to earn rewards. Badgeville supports two kinds of Activities widgets: site and user.

To display site activity:

```
<script id="badgeville_widget_activities"
src="http://api4.badgeville.com/api/555/widgets/activities"
type="text/javascript"></script>
```

To display achievement activity for a category:

```
<script id="badgeville_widget_activities" src="http://
api4.badgeville.com/api/555/widgets/activities
?tags=restaurant&session=currentusersessionid"
type="text/javascript"></script>
```

The tagged achievement activity example displays all restaurant-related rewards. You can show this information on a user profile page.

Skumo uses a vertical container that updates every few seconds to show an activity. For a large site, you can create a cron job to routinely update a cache that is used to populate the data in a responsive manner. Figure 8-14 shows an example.

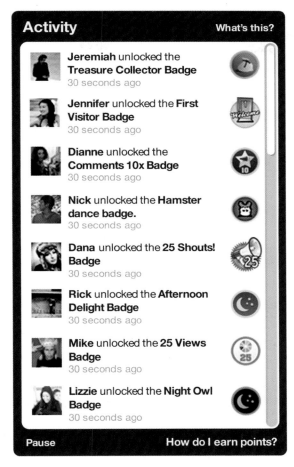

Figure 8-14. Example activity widget.

Step 10: Creating a Comment Widget

You can leverage rewards data in other systems on your site. For example, you can include a player's level, trophies, and total points in your comment system using a microwidget. You can create a comment microwidget using the API or by calling the Badgeville widget endpoint.

To show Badgeville data for a player in comments:

```
<script id="bv_widget_id"
src="http://api4.badgeville.com/api/555/widgets/comments?nickname=Test
User&embed_id=widget_id" type="text/javascript"></script>
```

In this example, you call the comment microwidget by using the widget's endpoint. You then specify the comment widget and the ID of the widget in the page where the comment will appear. The comment widget contains a level image, points total, and level name.

Enabling social-sharing

A modern rewards program leverages the social web. Here is an example of tracking Facebook-sharing by associating the Badgeville `bvCredit` function with the `onClick` event. You can use API calls or JavaScript to track sharing as long as the sharing button is not in an `iFrame`:

```
<a href='example' onclick='bvCredit("Share");'>Facebook Share!</a>
You can give credit for multiple behaviors in one call:
<a href='#' onclick='bvCredit("Share"); bvCredit("FBLike");'>Share!</a>
```

Facebook provides a Facebook Markup Language (FBML) version of the Like button that uses a JavaScript library. The example above uses that approach.

Analytics

Analytics is a key component to a loyalty and rewards program. How else will you know whether your programs are working and returning value? The Badgeville Publisher module provides statistics, reporting, and other tools to perform analysis (see Figure 8-15).

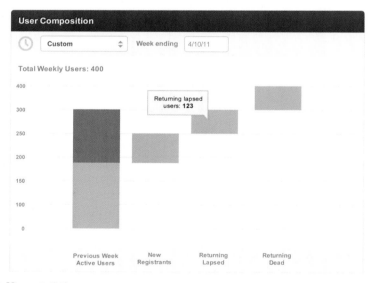

Figure 8-15. Usage statistics.

Badgeville has an engagement dashboard, which answers valuable questions like:

- Are you achieving your site objectives?
- Who are your most valuable users?
- What do your users like?
- What do your users not like?
- Who is sharing the most?
- Who is contributing the most?
- Who is creating the most conversations?

With proper analytics, you can determine which rewards are working and which are not, and adjust them accordingly.

Analyzing Sponsored Promotion Success

Here's a simple example. A few weeks after your site's launch, you view a motion chart of behavior trends. You notice that players aren't sharing as much as you anticipated. You decide to encourage sharing by finding a sponsor who will pay for the design and creation of a special badge, as well as the advertisement during the promotional period. Participants sharing reviews during the promotion earn the sponsored badge and a point bonus. After the promotional period ends, you use a motion chart to track activity trends. You stop the chart just before the promotion starts (see Figure 8-16), and you notice the rate of sharing prepromotion is 23 badges a day.

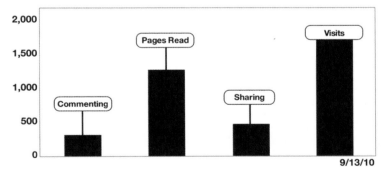

Figure 8-16. Sharing before the promotion.

You watch the chart during the days the promotion is active, and the rate of sharing accelerates rapidly (see Figure 8-17).

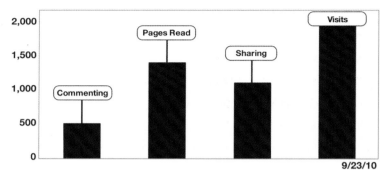

Figure 8-17. Sharing after the promotion.

In fact, while other behaviors increased consistently, sharing velocity tripled. To confirm, you run a report and compare two snapshots of sharing totals for two given days. Notice that you are not comparing page views or guessing player intent— you're analyzing meaningful interactions. Actionable insight is easier to get when the atomic unit of measurement is inherently more meaningful.

Getting Stats from the Badgeville API

If you already have a powerful analytics solution in place, you can query the Badgeville API to get statistics and usage data. Thus, if necessary, you can track the ROI of your loyalty and rewards program outside of Badgeville. From the API documentation, here's a snippet that explains the endpoint to query, as well as some of the data the service returns to support analytics.

Get statistics

Use this to get statistics related to Badgeville usage on the publisher site.

Route:

```
/api/publisher_id/publishers/stats
```

Receives:

```
PUBLISHER_ID: The publisher key.
```

The return is a JSON object with these totals, and more:

- Users registered for that publisher
- Number of new users registered in the last 24 hours
- Points earned by all the users of that publisher
- Points earned by all the users of that publisher in the last 24 hours

- Number of shares done by the users of that publisher
- Number of shares done by the users of that publisher in the last 24 hours
- Number of badges earned by the users of that publisher
- Number of badges earned by the users of that publisher in the last 24 hours

The returned code will look something like this, with the bracketed values filled in:

```
{"result"=>[boolean], "users"=>[integer], "today_users"=>[integer],
"points"=>[integer], "today_points"=>[integer], "shares"=>[integer],
"today_shares"=>[integer], "badges"=>[integer], "today_badges"=>[integer]}
```

The Game's Just Beginning

In this chapter, we attempted to show how you can leverage Badgeville's technology approach to game mechanics and rewards-program design to create engaging experiences that return a higher yield on customer interactions. Obviously, we barely scratched the surface. But the message should be clear: players want to be engaged, and they are flocking to sites that recognize and reward them. Using the methods described above, you can provide your players with this experience in just a matter of days or weeks. Individuals and companies who understand gamification and build it into their platforms will have a significant advantage in the coming battle for user engagement.

Index

About the Authors

Gabe Zichermann is the chair of the *Gamification Summit*—where top thought leaders in this burgeoning industry gather to share knowledge and insight. Zichermann is also an author, highly rated public speaker, and entrepreneur whose books, *Game-Based Marketing* (Wiley) and *Gamification by Design* (O'Reilly), look at the strategic business, technical, and architectural considerations for designing engagement using games concepts. A resident of NYC, Gabe is a board member of StartOut.org, advisor to a number of startups, and Facilitator for the Founder Institute in Manhattan. For more information about Gabe and gamification, visit the Gamification Blog at *http://gamification.co*.

Christopher Cunningham is an entrepreneur, author, and veteran technologist who has spent over a decade bringing innovative mobile and web products to market. He helped found rmbr, an early Gamification solution; beamME, a mobile social application; and TrekMail, a breakthrough mobile voice messaging application. He lives in Madrid, Spain, where he mentors several early-stage startups, speaks publicly on gamification and lean startup methodologies, and works as a consultant on mobile and web product strategy.

Colophon

The animal on the cover of *Gamification by Design* is the rhesus monkey (*Macaca mulatta*), a member of the macaque family. These animals are highly social, living in groups of 20 to 200 individuals where the female to male ratio can be as high as 4:1. In addition to this disparity, each gender has a separate hierarchy system within the group. Males—as in other animal species—gain dominance by age and experience, and young or defeated males are often driven away. In contrast, female rhesus monkeys have a stable matrilineal structure, wherein females inherit their rank from their mother. Even more uniquely in rhesus culture, younger daughters will also outrank their older sisters, likely because they are more fertile.

Rhesus monkeys have gray or brown fur and hairless pink faces, which are capable of displaying a large range of expressions. On average, their tails are 8–9 inches long, and they weigh 12–17 pounds. Native to South Asia and India, rhesus monkeys live in a wide range of terrain and altitudes, such as grassland, forests, and mountainous regions. They are most active during the day, and can be found in the trees, on the ground, or even swimming.

Fruit is the primary staple of their diet, but these monkeys also eat insects, seeds, and other plant matter. They are very adaptable, and have become notorious for stealing food (and other nonedible items that catch their interest) from urban areas.

Due to their large population and physiological similarity to humans, rhesus monkeys are often used in scientific research. Infant rhesus monkeys were test subjects in psychologist Harry Harlow's surrogate mother experiment, which studied the role that the mother-child bond (or lack thereof) has on development. In 1959, a rhesus monkey named Able earned the distinction of being one of the first two living beings to successfully return from outer space (the other was Miss Baker, a squirrel monkey on the same NASA mission). Able was preserved after his death, and is on display in the Smithsonian National Air and Space Museum.

Teresa Elsey and Adam Zaremba provided quality control for *Gamification by Design*. The book was composed in Adobe InDesign CS4 by Nancy Kotary.

The heading and text font is Myriad Pro, the code font is TheSansMonoCondensed, and the cover font is Gravur Condensed.

Have it your way.

Get even more for your money.

Join the O'Reilly Community, and register the O'Reilly books you own. It's free, and you'll get:

- $4.99 ebook upgrade offer
- 40% upgrade offer on O'Reilly print books
- Membership discounts on books and events
- Free lifetime updates to ebooks and videos
- Multiple ebook formats, DRM FREE
- Participation in the O'Reilly community
- Newsletters
- Account management
- 100% Satisfaction Guarantee

Signing up is easy:

1. Go to: oreilly.com/go/register
2. Create an O'Reilly login.
3. Provide your address.
4. Register your books.

Note: English-language books only

To order books online:
oreilly.com/store

For questions about products or an order:
orders@oreilly.com

To sign up to get topic-specific email announcements and/or news about upcoming books, conferences, special offers, and new technologies:
elists@oreilly.com

For technical questions about book content:
booktech@oreilly.com

To submit new book proposals to our editors:
proposals@oreilly.com

O'Reilly books are available in multiple DRM-free ebook formats. For more information:
oreilly.com/ebooks

Spreading the knowledge of innovators   oreilly.com